DEREK PARKER

THE
WEST COUNTRY

B. T. Batsford

London

To
Edna Charity
and
Lester Francis

First published 1973

© Derek Parker 1973

Text printed in Great Britain by Northumberland Press Ltd,
Gateshead, Co. Durham. Plates printed and books bound
by Richard Clay (The Chaucer Press) Ltd, Bungay, Suffolk,
for the publishers B. T. Batsford Ltd, 4 Fitzhardinge Street,
London W.1

ISBN 0 7134 0075 7

CONTENTS

LIST OF ILLUSTRATIONS

ACKNOWLEDGMENTS

The Author and Publisher would like to thank the following for permission to use photographs in this book: Peter Baker (2, 6, 16); Barnaby's Picture Library and David Bowen (20); J. Allan Cash (13); Noel Habgood (*frontispiece*, 4, 5, 7, 14, 19, 21); A. F. Kersting (8, 9, 12, 18) and Kenneth Scowen (3, 15, 16, 26).

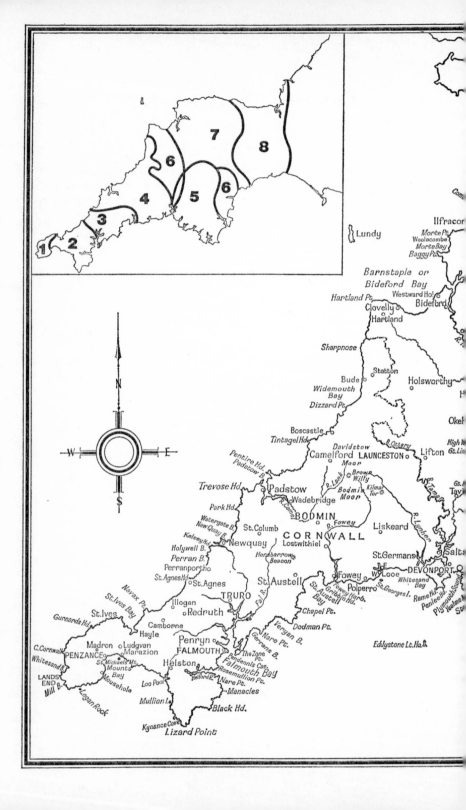

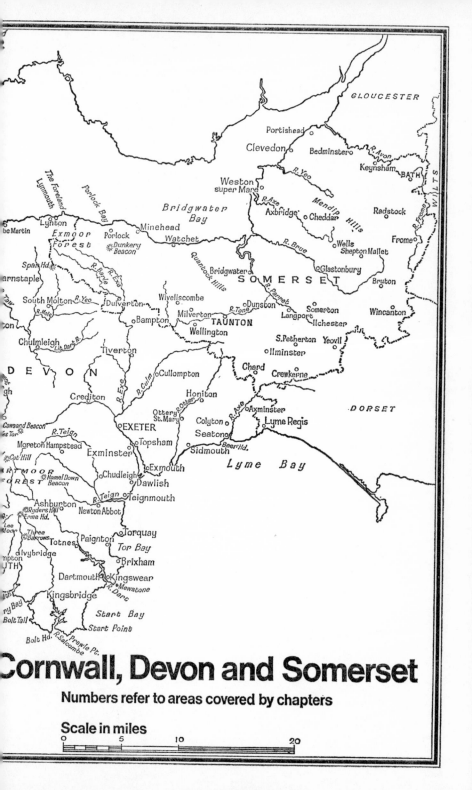

Cornwall, Devon and Somerset

Numbers refer to areas covered by chapters

Scale in miles

0   5   10   20

FOREWORD

Writing of Alexandria 50 years ago, E. M. Forster said: 'The best way to see it is to wander aimlessly about.' But that is a counsel of perfection. If one has only a fortnight or three weeks to spend in a place, one must have priorities, and the only way to discover them is to put oneself in the hands of someone who has been there before.

I try not to be too much the guide-book writer, however: to talk as much about the *style* of the countryside, of its history and its notable men and women, as about the number of miles from A to B, or of the number of bosses on the church roof. Anyone looking up a town in the index should find in the pages nearby some hints suggesting tours, or even walks, which will fill in an agreeable day.

Too often one reads on fly-leafs or in prefaces the claim that the author of a guide-book has travelled several thousands of miles to verify all the facts in his book; too often he is proved a liar very early indeed in the text. I have not revisited some of the places mentioned in this book for a good few years, and so there may be errors. I have however gone to some trouble to *attempt* to verify facts, and I hope the inaccuracies are few; I should be very glad to hear of them when they are found.

Every writer of any book of this kind must be greatly indebted to his predecessors; I am particularly grateful for two books—Claud Berry's *Cornwall* (Robert Hale, 1951), and W. G. Hoskins' *Devon* (Collins, 1954); while no writer, traveller, or amateur of architecture can but owe a great debt to Prof. Nikolaus Pevsner for his Penguin *Buildings of England* series. I am grateful to the poets Sir John Betjeman, Charles Causley and Jack Clemo for permission to quote from their work.

D.P.

CHAPTER ONE

The Penwith Peninsula

I was brought up on the assumption that 'we'—the Cornish—were somehow different from 'them'—anyone who lived east of the Tamar. We had to an even greater extent than the rest of the Celts, a fierce sense of topographical identity. The reference to the visitors (who, by the 'thirties, were already thronging almost every corner of the county) as 'foreigners' was not entirely a joke.

Now, in Cornwall, it is only the extremists (the members of Mebyon Kernow, still shouting seriously and in Cornish for Home Rule) who still insist on the separate identity of Cornwall and the Cornish people. And yet, Cornwall is in some respects unrelentingly un-English. Driving westward, it is still easier to tell precisely at what point one enters Cornwall than to tell when one is entering, say, Wales. There are several reasons for this, but the main one is topographical.

First—the sea. From Torpoint to Bude is, as the chough flies, a mere 60 miles, and to the westward the county narrows and narrows, until between Hayle and Marazion only six miles or so separate north coast from south coast. Nowhere, then—even, say, at Brown Willy, in the middle of the Bodmin Moor—is one far from the sea. A camper setting up his tent at a site apparently well inland will hear, in the middle of the night, the slow pounding of a subdued pulse: Atlantic breakers rolling in to thump at the foot of cliffs miles away.

And there is another sense than its purely physical presence, in which the sea has set the Cornish apart from the English. Around the Cornish coast between the seventeenth century and the middle of the twentieth, over 800 sizable ships have crashed on to the rocks—as well as innumerable unrecorded smaller vessels. *La Victoire, Jonkheer Meester V de Wall*, the *Montreal Packet, Nostra*

Sencra de Boa; the *Torrey Canyon*; the *Warspite*; two English sub-
marines, and 14 German U-boats ... the list is formidable, and linked
with the clusters of rock—the Manacles, the Shark's Fin, the Wolf
—which have made the first sight of the Cornish coast a dismal one
for thousands of sailors, and their passengers.

As a first sight of England on a calm, sunny summer's day, the
cliffs of west Cornwall are magical : exactly like an Arthur Rackham
drawing, so that one scans them eagerly for the towers and pinnacles of an Arthurian castle, and watches delighted as the little
white-washed houses glide past, flashing briefly in the sun from the
green crevices which hide the south coast villages—Porthcurno, Per-
ranuthnoe, Porthlevan, Mullion.... But anyone who has seen this
same coast from the sea in a storm is unlikely ever to look at it
again with the same pleasure. A full gale from the south-west sends
terrible breakers growling almost to the top of the cliffs, the wind
hissing in unstoppably from the Atlantic, so that the crew of the
Lizard Lifeboat used to crawl on hands and knees to their boat-house,
for fear of being blown clear over the cliff.

But there are storms on other coasts, as violent if perhaps not as
dangerous. The word which made a Cornish storm particularly
menacing to seamen was 'wreckers'. By the middle of the nineteenth
century, legends of wrecking on the Cornish coasts—of the luring of
ships on to the rocks by the use of false signals during storms—
had become so common that exemplary sentences were being passed,
to show the rest of England that the Cornish magistrates were conscious of the problem. When the barque *Duke of Clarence* ran ashore
in Whitesand Bay (between Looe and Rame Head) in 1846, an un-
fortunate young fisherman was sent down for a long term of hard
labour for stealing a short length of iron chain. He had had nothing
to do with the wreck, of course.

In fact, there is little evidence of wrecking on these coasts. There
was one suspicious case—of a Virginian trader which struck the
rocks near St. Agnes, in the Isles of Scilly, in 1680. The lighthouse-
keeper had carefully set out his light to warn her, but five minutes
after he had heard her sides crunch on the rocks. He, the Scillonians
were quick to point out, was a Cornishman; and as a direct result,
Trinity House issued an order that no Cornishman should be employed again at that light.

The Cornish reputation for wrecking was based, it seems, on nothing more than rumour, bolstered by the general taciturnity and unpredictability of the Cornish, and on the fact that they had a language of their own, and therefore were clearly not to be trusted. This historical reason cut them off in the same way as the Welsh or the Scots from commerce with ordinary decent English folk. Then, long after the Cornish language had ceased to be in general use, Cornwall came out solidly for the King in the English civil war, whereas the rest of the West Country was for Parliament. A traditional enmity between Cornwall and Plymouth can be directly traced to the time when the city was surrounded by Royalists, and a Parliamentary army lay there under siege. Many Plymouthians today still deeply mistrust the Cornish—to the extent that some of them decline to use the new road bridge over the Tamar, and prefer instead to queue for the car ferry. The chains hauling that across from Plymouth to Torpoint could in an emergency be cut: the Cornish, capable of everything from wrecking to Royalist sympathies, should be distanced.

The casual visitor arriving in Cornwall for a summer holiday is unlikely to come to the immediate conclusion that a wrecker lives in every other cottage, or that civil war is about to break out with Devonshire. But he will certainly be aware soon after he crosses the Tamar Bridge, or drives through Launceston (where the A30, the other main road from England, enters the county) that he has arrived at somewhere particularly un-English; and although I am by nature anti-nationalistic, it must be said again that, quite seriously, Cornwall is like nowhere else in the country, not only for the reasons I have given, but for purely physical reasons. The place itself is unique: every village, every ruined minehead, the small fields tucked in folds of the hills, the towering hedges, all recall the time when the county was physically isolated from the rest of England, and cut off by the sea from Europe and the rest of the world. The towering cliffs on all sides (only temporarily interrupted by a few gentle sloping beaches and protected coves), underline this solitariness; and the slate or granite shelves which rise from the coast to the bare and wind-swept uplands of the central moors—of the Land's End peninsula, of the Lizard, or further east—give the countryside a remote and inaccessible atmosphere.

2 *St. Ives, the harbour and St. Ia's Church*

But the deep valleys which cut into these plateaux and moorlands, are sheltered wooded crevices into which the sea often runs to form beautiful estuaries, unexpectedly leading the casual motorist down to some sandy bay where a sheltered camping-ground, or some bed-and-breakfast cottage (for the county has not entirely succumbed to the plastic horror of the main holiday centres such as Newquay) will welcome him. And if he chooses to stay there, he can walk during one easy day's relaxation over the cliffs to downs punctured by neglected tin-mines, through farms and tiny hamlets, and over a landscape where it is easier to trace the history of the ground beneath his feet than perhaps anywhere else in the British Isles.

He may come to a megalithic *fogou*, or artificial cave, built of vast granite boulders, so ancient that it has not yet been dated— and a few steps further on, pass a Cornish cross around which a Celtic farmer shaped his fields. Four miles from an Anglo-Saxon village, he can buy (if he is specially fortunate) a genuine, unimported Cornish pasty for his lunch, and eat it on the quay of a medieval fishing-port before dining in an hotel completed in the 1970s.

The Celtic influence on the landscape is very strong: at almost every crossroad there will be a tiny group of houses—only two or three, with perhaps a pub and a church. Sometimes a church will appear, tucked at the side of a hill, or (more likely) breasting the Atlantic winds from its top, the rectory crumbling at its side—and no other building in sight: only open farmland of mixed pasture or arable land, with small irregularly shaped fields bordered by walls of granite slabs or slates. But the remoteness is no more than an impression, for behind that clump of trees, around the corner of that swelling breast of hill, will be a farmhouse with a narrow lane, hidden by hedges so tall that they join across the track to make a tunnel leading to the nearest main road.

This pattern of tiny fields and isolated small settlements is particularly typical of Cornwall; although of course it is not general. Particularly in the east and north-east—around Lostwithiel, Bodmin and St. Austell, and up to Launceston around the borders of the Bodmin Moor—the fields become, often, narrower and more like the strips typical of Anglo-Saxon farming. This was the part of the county most nearly affected by the civilising English influence in the

3   *Godfrey Lighthouse, guarding the east point of St. Ives Bay*

Middle Ages, and the isolated villages are larger and more compact than in the west.

The other permanent signs of history are those of any other county: medieval castle, Elizabethan manor house, ancient bridge and church, nineteenth-century nonconformist chapel ... these tell the story of Cornwall just as they tell the story of Warwickshire or Hertfordshire; even if the story is still, somehow, different.

Let us start a more particular account of the county at the Land's End. Most people who come to Cornwall visit Land's End once; which is a good reason why once is enough. In winter the landscape still has tremendous grandeur, especially if one walks around the cliffs southward towards the Logan Rock. Then, on a clear day, the slate-grey sea and sky have a vast imponderability which is unforgettable; and on a rough day breaker after breaker driven by Atlantic winds contrives to make even the solid granite cliffs vibrate. It is not difficult to visualise the *Nereid* driving ashore here in 1797, to become an unrecognisable mass of wooden fragments before anyone could reach her; or an old fisherman watching as the sails of the *Khyber* were torn ragged to stream away in the wind from her broken masts, before she split her bottom open and sank.

On a lucky day, a visit to the westernmost tip of England can be memorable; on an unlucky day (and every moderately fine day between June and September is likely to be unlucky) the visitor will find himself confronted by a sea of fellow tourists, hemmed in by fleets of char-à-bancs, and pestered to buy plastic pixies and miniature granite lighthouses until he might be forgiven for thinking that the entire landscape had been put together overnight by a firm of enterprising local scene-shifters.

Describing Land's End is a task I prefer on the whole to avoid: in some senses it is precisely as one expects it to be, and in others (commercialisation apart) more splendid. But physical descriptions of landscape are best left to writers of genius; it is very easy to sound ridiculous, and when I am tempted to superlatives, I always remember the awful example of one Baker Peter Smith, whose *A Trip to the Far West* is an example of Victorian topographical writing at its most full-blown. Having observed 'the multicapsular curiosities of the region', he stands on the utmost peak of granite, and concludes:

4 *St. Mawes Castle: built by Henry* VIII

'The entranced spectator has no election, but is engrossed with admiration of that Great Power by the fiat of whose mere volition nature's chaos was thus harmonised and stamped with the glorifying impress of multiplicious beauty.'

One's best recourse in the face of Land's End at the height of the season is to turn off the main road at any one of many little lanes, and to wait for something interesting to come into view. A large-scale map of the area, if he is that kind of driver, will prove even more invaluable here than elsewhere in England, for there is something interesting at every turn—usually hidden behind high hedges —and usually something as old as it is interesting. In Neolithic, Bronze and Iron Ages, Land's End peninsula was an absolute stronghold of tribes. Palaeolithic man lived here, of course: but not many of him. Somehow, at the beginning of the Neolithic period (about 2500 B.C.) a stream of people seems to have made for this part of the country: because they had few good tools, they left the wooded areas severely alone, and made for the balder higher areas where building materials lay around, ready to hand.

The traces they left are often very odd: the only ones still fully understood are the quoits—massive upright posts of granite supporting a crossbeam: not like those at Stonehenge, for these crossbeams form a roof, and three or even four sides are closed in, so that the monuments (as the historian Norden pointed out three centuries ago) look like 'little howses raysed of mightie stones, standing on a little hill within a fielde.' There are two particularly splendid ones: Lanyon Quoit (about three miles from Penzance, at Madron) and Trevethy Quoit (at St. Cleer, at the other end of the county).

The quoits were, of course, tombs, once covered by mounds of earth, which have been worn away by four thousand years of wind and weather—one quoit, near Helston, the Beacon Hut, is still partly covered. It seems likely that the Cornish plundered the quoits for their granite slabs, which were broken up and used for hedging (some granite boulders which form parts of Cornish hedges make one wonder how on earth they could have been placed in position). The circles of granite stones which also dot the landscape seem to have been left severely alone, perhaps because of the legends which collected around them, and which still today are remarkably potent— the Nine Maidens at Boscawen Un (at St. Buryan, on the B3283 from

Penzance to Land's End) are nine granite posts, once living, warm girls turned to stone for dancing on the Sabbath.

The legends have additional potency because the real purpose of the circles can only be guessed. As Norden put it, looking at the Hurlers (at St. Cleer), men metamorphosed for hurling on a Sunday : 'This monumente seemeth to importe an intention of the memoriall of some matter ... thowgh time have worne out the maner.' My own feeling is that these monuments (often grouped together in twos and threes, and mainly on the Land's End peninsula and the Bodmin Moor) are most likely to have something to do with astronomy— with the prediction of eclipses and other celestial events—in the same way in which other British ancient monuments have been so persuasively linked with astronomical intentions by Professor A. Thom, in his fascinating book *Megalithic Lunar Observatories*.

Even more mysterious than the standing stones and circles are the *fogous*. I well remember, when I was a junior reporter on *The Cornishman* (the weekly newspaper which still serves West Cornwall) being dispatched to the parish of Sancreed, where an unsuspecting farmer had just fallen into an unsuspected hole in the ground, which turned out to be a *fogou*. But as to the purpose or origin of the hole, I was unable to discover very much; and indeed this is still difficult. *Fogous*, often lined by slabs of stone even more massive than the quoits, are clustered about the Penwith peninsula—at St. Buryan, St. Just, Sancreed, Madron, Zennor, Mawgan-in-Meneage.... Burial chambers? This seems the obvious solution; and yet perhaps they were not, for they seem too elaborate : dry-walled caves, roofed with lintel stones, with more than one entrance, a main passage giving way to small rooms, and often with low, narrow side-passages through which one must creep like a snake on one's belly.... Then there are the 'trap' passages, which look as though they lead from the *fogou* to the air, but which after a turn or two end in a scree of carefully placed wall-stones. It is all very odd.

The word *fogou* seems to derive, in the ancient Cornish, from *fo* (a flight or retreat) and *gow* (false, deceitful, hidden). Perhaps, then, a place for hiding from one's enemies, and for luring them to their deaths. It is this proposition which has seemed to me to be most likely to be true, as I have crouched uncomfortably in the damp, dark corner of one of these earthy, unearthly caverns. Many of them have been destroyed, but some remain to be explored, though carefully. Perhaps the most spectacular is at Chapel Euny, in Sancreed parish; it has a splendid circular chamber, a Bronze Age passage-grave nearby, the remains of a shrine (to St. Euny?) near a spring not far away, and for those for whom *fogous* provide not more than half an hour's interest, the site is wonderfully placed, with the most glorious views over both southern and western coasts.

I once overheard a disgusted small boy protesting from a sweltering Mini that he was bored stiff with Cornwall because there was 'nothing but *country*'. He was not alone: William Gilpin, that intrepid traveller (certainly most travellers of his time were intrepid, but he was more intrepid than most) once travelled to Cornwall, but got no further than Bodmin, for (he said) he saw nothing but 'a barren and naked country, in all respects as uninteresting as can well be conceived', and was told that west of Bodmin things did not improve; in fact, they got worse. Well, indeed, this is true: but the wildest parts of West Cornwall have their rewards, as the naturalist W. H. Hudson saw. His description of the Land's End peninsula as it was in 1908 will do today:

'The black, frowning, wave-beaten cliffs on the one hand, the hills and moors on the other, treeless, strewn abundantly with granite boulders, rough with heath and furze and bracken, the summits crowned with great masses of rock resembling ancient ruined castles. Midway between the hills and the sea, half a mile or so from the cliffs, are the farms, but the small houses and walled fields on the inhabited strip hardly detract from the rude and savage aspect of the country. Nature will be Nature here, and man, like the other inhabitants of the wilderness, has adapted himself to the conditions. The badgers have their earths, the foxes their caverns in the rocks, and the linnets, yellow-hammer, and magpie hide their nests, big and little, in the dense furze bushes: he in like manner builds his dwelling small and low, sheltering as best he can in any slight depression in the ground, or behind thickets of furze and the rocks he piles up....'

It is never mild country here, even when the sun shines, though in sheltered corners of the moors open exhibitions of flowers can be found, 12 or 13 species at a time—most of them, it seems, blue! —surrounded by ramparts of gorse, a glittering yellow in spring.

I have concentrated so much on the countryside of the Penwith peninsula because the villages are really in themselves of little interest: except inasmuch as they seem to grow out of the very earth and granite which surrounds them, as bleak as the very cliffs. Yet they preserve their individuality, if only because of the quick shifts of atmosphere which characterise the areas of countryside around them. Dr. William Borlase compared the districts of Ludgvan and St. Just, near neighbours: 'In the former I have all the pleasures of a southern sun, a fine valley, a bay with a gently declining shore, trading towns, prettily planted villages, and now the Spring is come, all vegetable nature awake. In the latter there is one perpetual hue of heath, no tree to blossom nor shrub to flower. The bleak northern sea is edged by steep and craggy cliffs, the hills and valleys equally bestrewed with rocks; and what seemingly adds to the natural horror of the places is, that you everywhere meet with little growing mountains of rubbish, which are thrown up here out of tin mines, and would be so many blemishes and deformities on any other surface than this.' Borlase's old friend and correspondent, P. A. S. Pool, compared Ludgvan in return to 'a buxom girl of 18, always laughing and playing', and St. Just to 'an old, haggard philosopher'.

St. Just-in-Penwith, Sennen, St. Buryan—none of them are of engrossing interest. They all have their churches (Sennen's the westernmost in England) with typically sturdy towers generally cornered with granite—and granite too makes most of the cottages built before the turn of the last century entirely typical of the area. There has never been much wood available for building in West Cornwall (precious little in the rest of the county, for that matter). So one finds no half-timbered cottages; most of them were built of cob (two parts mud, one part odd bits and pieces of slate). There is no sign of brick before 1700.

So for the larger houses, the Cornish builders used stone, and stone meant granite. The silver-grey buildings which shimmer in the bright sunshine seem in summer as in winter a natural and organic part of the landscape. The Cornish are used to the medium: they have used it since the Bronze Age, and on every side one finds it, strengthening the wall of a church, bridging a stream, or (once the masons learned how to dress it properly) making neat stone fronts to domestic houses. By Georgian times, considerable refinement was possible: the Vicarage at Lostwithiel shows just how elegant granite could appear.

Slate was another matter: not as strong as granite, of course, but admirable for roofing—and exported for that purpose as early as the twelfth century, from quarries like the giant one at Delabole, which is still worth visiting. Cornish roofs are perhaps the best and sturdiest, still, in England.

Anyone particularly interested in building materials will find some odd ones appearing in the interior of some Cornish houses: polyphant and serpentine, for instance, elvan and catacleuse—all mined in the county, and used for decoration in 'great houses' at Trerice, Anthony, Trewithen and Place. But at the Land's End, all is granite and slate; the houses needed to be strong above all, to be able to put a brave front on the Atlantic storms; and strong they are.

In many of them lived, until a mere 50 years ago, a strong breed of men: the Cornish tin miners. Stand on the hill above Botallack, between St. Just and Pendeen, and below you lies the most famous of the Cornish tin mines, its ruined engine house 30 feet above the sea, under which the galleries ran, so that miners could hear the tides knocking against the thin rock walls above them.

Celia Fiennes (who travelled *Through England on a Side Saddle* in the 1880s) found that at least 20 tin mines could be seen at one time, with more than 1,000 men at work in them, the ore being drawn to the surface in leather buckets, then pounded to a powder and heated in a fire until it ran molten into trenches below. The mines were spread throughout the western half of Cornwall, up through the Camborne-Redruth area; and while they provided a great deal of work (what was there else, other than fishing?) they also provided a considerable amount of misery. William Beckford (the eccentric author of *Vathek*) went in 1787 to Gwennap, and returned to Falmouth horrified by the blackness of the pits into which the miners descended—pits linked with the surface only by shaky ladders, and with 'warm, copperous vapours' threatening to stifle the men, who lived in tiny huts at the mineheads, hardly able even to afford bread, let alone meat, and frequently dying of tuberculosis or silicosis. As late as 1920 most miners earned little more than £2 a week; no wonder the area has always been radical in politics!

But at least one can thank the miners for the invention of one of the famous Cornish dishes: the pasty. Instead of wrapping their lunchtime snack in a cloth, the miners' wives wrapped it in pastry (on which they then marked a cross with their thumbnail, to keep away the piskies which lived in the bottomless shafts—the 'knockers' whose faint signals were the counterparts of Tennyson's horns of elfland faintly blowing). The pastry was then baked; and the traditional test of a good pasty was to drop it down the deepest shaft of the mine. If, at the bottom, it remained unbroken, then it was 'vitty'.

A quick word about the pasty: it consists of beef, cut into small pieces, and wrapped in pastry with *raw* potato, also cut small; perhaps some turnip; possibly some onion; and baked. In Cornwall, one asks the butcher for 'pasty meat': entrecote will do. But refuse all imitations, containing for instance *minced* meat! As for tinned pasty, which one has seen on sale ... there are no words in the English language to describe such blasphemy!

As recently as 1926, Cornwall provided over a million pounds worth of tin in one year. The industry began to fall off in the 1930s, picked up a little during the Second World War, but then declined almost to nothing. In the deep flooded tin mines there are still millions of pounds worth of tin; but although attempts are being made to re-establish the industry in the country, this has been found economically difficult because the deposits are apparently too deep to compete with more easily available ore from elsewhere. There is one Cornish stream works in the Portreath Valley (two miles from Redruth) where a museum contains much of the old mining machinery, and where tin is produced from beach sand and from waste left by the old miners. The Tolgus tin works and museum are open from Easter Monday until the end of October, or by appointment at other times. It is an interesting if melancholy memorial to an industry which through emigration supplied the world's mining industry with thousands of highly skilled workers. 'Wherever there's a hole in the ground, you'll find a Cornishman at the bottom of it', it was said.

The ruined engine-houses of the tin mines, like desolate castles of the long-dead race of Cornish giants, rise behind many a mill. They are best seen—so are the church towers, the little granite cottages, indeed most of the features of the Cornish landscape—not from the main road, but from the open country. In the past 20 or 30 years many roads in the county have been widened; many hedges torn down. But the more remote parts of Cornwall are still to be reached only by very narrow lanes through which a motorist must be prepared to back for a mile or so in front of an oncoming rural 'bus.

But I assume that anyone really wishing to explore Cornwall will not mind walking for a few miles. The chances of being able to hire a horse are not very great; and the old days of the donkey-shay are gone, alas—though I can remember rattling along the lanes in one of those precarious but delightful equipages; one was just high enough to see over the top of the grasses.

No, walking is the answer; and happily there is a footpath now round the whole of the coastline, from which one can see the county at its best, and in several moods; it provides some of the most spectacular views in the county, and on a fine day, the colours of the sea are breathtaking. Homer's wine-coloured Mediterranean is rivalled by the Cornish sea, where it becomes shallow over sea-weeded rocks and turns claret-coloured; elsewhere, light green darkening to olive, mulberry, almost black. Above the water the gulls (of which, more later) and the voracious gannet (I was accused as a child of 'eating like a gannet') with its strong, pointed, black-tipped wings, pauses in mid-flight to fall, drawing a flashing line in a vertical 25-foot drop to the sea, and sending a splash of water eight or ten feet into the air as it thuds through the surface to harpoon a fish with its beak : a startling and memorable sight.

One would be lucky, these days, to see a chough, though it is Cornwall's emblem, and appears on the county's coat-of-arms. Occasionally, one will wander into its own land, and make a minor headline in a local newspaper. More slender than a crow, it has a red beak and red legs, its plumage is tinged with green, and it is reputed to be Merlin in disguise, keeping an eye open for favourable conditions to reawaken great Arthur.

South of Land's End, the footpath leads first to Porthgwarra, a tiny fishing village, so insignificant still that scarcely any guide-book mentions it; the cliffs above it seem almost to offer it directly to the sea; but in fact it is a pleasantly sheltered place of considerable charm. Once, many Cornish fishing villages must have shared this kind of obscurity; now, none of them do. The only parallel I can think of is the tiny hamlets on the shores of Gozo (which indeed is not unlike West Cornwall, except in climate).

Farther on, Porthcurno, best known outside the county for its Cable and Wireless Station, but inside the county for the Minack Theatre, opened in 1932 by Miss Rowena Cade, who hacked it out of the cliffside at the bottom of her garden, with her own hands; and is still building it, on and off. An amphitheatre high over the sea, the Minack has been described as 'the most beautiful theatre in Europe'. This is pitching it a little high. But on a summer's night, as one sits above the grassy stage with the dark sea and sky behind it, watching perhaps *The Tempest*, or a performance of ballet or opera (or, indeed, *Charley's Aunt* or *The Drunkard*, for the Minack programme is varied) it is easy to believe so, for the whole of nature seems to combine to make the performances memorable. I have seen *King Lear* here in a thunderstorm (and very uncomfortable it was, too); watched a sail round the headland just as Kurwenal announced the sight of Isolde's ship to the dying Tristan; seen Ariel, set free, dive into the sea like a gannet from the farthest rock of the bay. There are performances here, now, every year. One hint: take a car-rug and a thermos—the Cornish Riviera can get pretty chilly by eleven in the evening.

On along the cliff path to the nearby Logan Rock: balanced, all 60 tons of it, clumsily upon another stone. At one time, it could be stirred by virtually a finger's weight. It takes more than that to stir it now. In the 1820s, prompted by the local legend that it could not be toppled (and that something extremely unpleasant would happen to Cornwall, England, perhaps the world, if it was!) a Lieut. Goldsmith led 12 sturdy wreckers up the cliff, and tipped the Logan Rock off its perch.

The world went rolling on; but the infuriated Cornish immediately raised a fund for the stone's replacement, and it was laboriously hoisted back into place before any occult disaster had struck. But things were not the same: one had to get one's back under the stone to move it at all, and it still only provides a faint shudder after a great deal of effort.

Farther east along the cliff path is Lamorna, famous as an artists' colony long before St. Ives: Lamorna Birch probably did most to popularise it in painstaking, luminous, traditional landscapes. Who remembers this gentle old man and good painter now? But Lamorna remains, and is relatively unspoiled: in spring, a mass of wild flowers, sheltered by hazels and alders. Somewhere behind the trees, at the bottom of the valley, one can hear a stream and perhaps a waterfall; but shrubs, ferns, brambles prevent one from reaching it. There is a little pier of—of course—granite, cut no doubt from the quarry just behind it, from which in 1851 a block 22-feet high and weighing 21 tons was made into an obelisk and sent off to London to the Great Exhibition. What *can* have become of it?

Up the hill; over a field; and below one lies Mousehole, one of those Cornish villages whose enchantment is oddly incorporeal. Not a single house of any quality; no special beauty of design; just a little muddle of houses tacked around the edge of a tiny harbour, and —perhaps this is the secret—too small and too protected by the contours of the country for modern development to touch it.

To Mousehole, Dylan Thomas brought his bride, Caitlin Macnamara, after their marriage in July, 1937, in a registry office in Penzance, 'with no money; no prospect of money; no attendant friends or relatives, and in complete happiness.' They still remember Dylan in some of the pubs around here, stumping off in his bottle-green overcoat, the bottles of stout clinking in the vast pockets, to be drunk in the circle of the minute cinema in Penzance which was his favourite haunt on a wet afternoon.

A good time to be in Mousehole, and if possible snug inside the warm walls of the Ship Inn, is on Tom Bawcock's Eve—December 23. Tom Bawcock was a Mousehole fisherman who put to sea after a great dearth of fish, so that the village was literally starving. The only man with sufficient faith to put out, Bawcock returned with enough fish to satisfy the hunger of everyone in the community, and has been celebrated ever since in a song. And here it is, for it will form as good an introduction as any to a rumination about the Cornish dialect and language:

> *A merry place you may believe*
> *Was Mouzel on Tom Bawcock's Eve;*
> *To be there then who wudn' wish*
> *To sup on sebn sorts o' fesh.*

When morgy brath had cleared the path
Comed lances for a fry,
And then us had a bit o' scad
An' starey gazy pie.

Next comed fermaads, bra' thusty jades
As made out oozles dry,
An' ling an' hake, enough to make
A rauning shark to sigh.

As aich we'd clunk a's health were drunk
In bumpers brimmin' high,
An' when up came Tom Bawcock's name
We praised un to the sky.

The first verse, I suppose, presents no difficulty : *sebn* is of course the Cornish equivalent of *seven*, and the soft *e* making *fish* an altogether more affectionate noun. A *morgy* is a dogfish, good only for making broth; and a *starey gazy pie*, or sometimes *starry-gazy*, is a splendid dish of pilchards in a pie, laid with their tails to the centre, their heads protruding through the pastry and gazing outwards, or maybe upwards at the stars?

Fermaads have nothing to do with fair maids, or mermaids; they are pilchards from which the oil has been squeezed, and they are generally grilled like kippers. They used once to be smoked; but no longer. One's *oozle* is one's windpipe, and the shark in the third verse is not running but *ravening*. To *clunk* is to *swallow*.

That is just one example of preserved dialect; but these preservations are as much for the sake of the tourists as through any genuine affection. I am sometimes under the impression indeed that Cornish dialect speech is dying out even more rapidly than dialects elsewhere in Britain; partly because of the universal effect of radio, partly because of the continuing effects of travel. Here and there, enthusiasts purposely keep alive the sound of the Cornish dialect which even 30 years ago was much more common than it is today. Others, mainly members of the Gorseth Kernow (an offspring of the Welsh Gorsedd) study the ancient Cornish language, the literature of which a century ago seemed doomed to oblivion, because so few people could read or write the language. The late R. Morton Nance almost single-handed was responsible for resuscitating Cornish (a language with points in common with Gaelic, Welsh and Breton), and the Gorseth now holds examinations in its grammar and syntax, in writing and speech.

Cornish itself died out many centuries ago: even Norden found that 'of late the Cornishe men have much conformed themselves to the use of the Englishe toung, and their Englishe is equall to the beste.' Well, among the upper classes this may have been so; but among the cottagers it was certainly not the case, even recently. I remember as a child the difficulty English visitors often had in understanding ordinary conversation in the vernacular. Andrew Borde in his *Boke of the Introduction of Knoledge*, in 1542, was nearer the mark than Norden when he wrote: 'In Cornwall is two speeches, the one is naughty Englische, and the other Cornysshe speeche.' Naughty English is what almost every Cornish villager spoke, as late as the 1920s—a speech, as one Cornish historian pointed out, 'the peculiarity of which was a striking uncertainty of the speaker as to where one word left off and another began'. Now more than likely, a Cornishman who addresses a visitor in dialect will (unless he is over 70) have studied to preserve it, and among his family will be very easily understood by an eavesdropper.

It is worth digressing for a moment to speak of the Cornish language itself, however: there can be few parcels of land whose inhabitants have retained their original language, even if only vestigially. Of course you will not find Cornish spoken in everyday conversation, these days; this has not happened for centuries. Richard Carew, writing at the very beginning of the seventeenth century (in his *Survey of Cornwall*) found that already English had driven the local language into nooks and corners, and that 'most of the inhabitants can speak no word of Cornish, but very few are ignorant of the English'. But with the tenacious individualism which shows itself now in the fringe movements demanding home rule and a Parliament at Truro, the sixteenth-century Cornishman continued to pray in his own language, and 'some so affect their own as to a stranger they will not speak [English], for if meeting them by chance you inquire the way or any such matter, your answer shall be *Meea navidna cowzasawkech, I can speak no Saxonage*'.

Especially for a Cornishman who speaks no Cornish, it is strange to listen to a Gorsedd, or perhaps to a play or recitation in Cornish—the intonation is so strongly that of the *dialect*, the very sound of the vowels so familiar, that one feels one *should* understand it, even when it is patently beyond one's reach. Mr. Morton Nance translated many miracle plays and moralities into English, and very good they are too; it is grateful that the language does still live. And here for a taste of it is the Cornish version of *The Twelfth Day of Christmas*. It is not a precise translation of the English version, for it runs:

'Twelve days after Christmas my true love said to me: twelve ships a-sailing, eleven bulls a-bleating, ten ladies dancing, nine lords leaping, eight deer a-running, seven swans a-swimming, six geese a-laying, five gold rings, four Cornish birds, three French hens, two turtle-doves, pass through a juniper tree.'

And the Cornish:

> *Gol an Steren yn meth ow huf-colon dhymmo-vy:*
> *Deudhek lester ow-mora,*
> *Unnek tarow owth-uja,*
> *Dek arlodhes ow-tonsya*
> *Naw arluth ow-lamma,*
> *Eth carow ow-ponya,*
> *Seyth alargh ow-nyja,*
> *Whegh goth ow-tedhwy,*
> *Pymp bysow owr,*
> *Peder edhen Kernewek,*
> *Tyr yar Frynkek,*
> *Dyw duren,*
> *Ha grugyar awarth'yn gwedhen per.*

The pronunciation of the language (as with Welsh) has rubbed off on the English which succeeded it, and although BBC English is making severe inroads, the Cornish speech still remains pleasant and warm, its warmth almost physical, for it is a soft and almost embracing sound.

The visitor will notice a considerable difference between the east Cornish dialect, and the west Cornish: perhaps the dialect of the

Land's End peninsula is the warmer (the bad influence of Devon creeping in, no doubt!) There are some factors which are common to both, and peculiar to Cornish: the *s* at the beginning of words becoming a soft burry *z* is most familiar, and most used by repertory actors playing any character supposed to be at home anywhere west of the Chiswick flyover. *Zeem* for *seem*; *zolid* for *solid*. *F* in the same way becomes *v*: *vish* for *fish*; *vollow* for *follow*. *Th* will sometimes be pronounced *d*, so you may hear 'I'm going dreshing', for 'I'm going threshing'. And as far as the English language itself is concerned, the elderly Cornishman will sometimes, though decreasingly, become confused about the past tense: 'I knowed that', he will say; or 'I gove it him' rather than 'I gave it him'. And occasionally words ending in a mute consonant will undergo a metamorphosis, so that a potato crisp will end up as a potato crips.

The greatest pity of all perhaps is that some of the West Country coinage is vanishing: even those common to Devon and Cornwall. How vividly *airy-mouse* brings to mind a bat; how inspiriting to give one's child a *larripping* because he is a *mazegerry*, rather than to wallop him because he is thoughtless. A *plashet* is patently a damp piece of ground where a spring rises; a near thing is *nibby-gibby*, and anyone who drinks quickly is *gaddling*.

The Cornish antiquary Davies Gilbert recorded many splendid Cornish sayings. He was once on the bench when a man was brought before him on a charge of poisoning a neighbour, and a witness spoke of the loaf of bread which was said to contain the poison.

Gilbert: Did you see anything in the loaf?
Witness: Yes. When I cut it open, I found it full of treade.
Gilbert: Treade? What is that?
Witness: Oh, it's ropes-ends, dead mice, and other combustibles.

However, to return to Mousehole: while one is in the area, a walk up the hill to Paul will prove exhausting but pleasant, not only for the view, but for the sake of making a pilgrimage to the grave of Dolly Pentreath, who died in 1778, and was said (inaccurately) to have been the last person to have spoken the Cornish language and no other. (There is another monument in the churchyard with an inscription partly in Cornish.)

Paul church, and most of Mousehole, was burned down by the Spaniards during a sudden raid in 1595. While the Penzance people cowered behind their shutters, watching the red glow to the south, and waiting their turn—which indeed came soon enough—most of the villagers of Mousehole were slaughtered. There used, years ago, to be an inscription on the Church wall: 'The Spanzer burnt this Church in the year 1595.' The parish register records the event and its fatalities: 'Jenkin Keigwin of Mousehole, being killed by the Spaniards, was buried ye 24 of Julii 1595.'

Before looking at Penzance, back to the Land's End and the footpath to the north, around Cape Cornwall and towards St. Ives. The walk from the Land's End around Cape Cornwall towards Gurnards Head is one of the loveliest in the county: more beautiful, if less full of incident, than the southern path.

It follows the sweep of the coastline, passing north of Pendeen (with a church built in 1851 by its parishioners, to their parson's design!) before turning south to join the road at Morvah, a little hamlet surrounded on all sides by prehistoric remains—including Chun Castle, the only stone-built fort in the county, with ramparts ten feet high, and as impressive as the Cornish hedges.

Talking of hedges, here is another peculiarly Cornish feature of this landscape: in much of England, economics have forced farmers to tear down their hedges and make their fields ever-larger, so that in most counties a field no longer bears any relation to the small individual strip of land associated with the small farmsteads of medieval times. In Cornwall, however, the landscape dictates otherwise. With the countryside taking it into its head to dive at any moment down a seven-in-one incline, or up to an inland cliff, the fields must be small, and hedges necessary not only to mark one from the other, but to prevent cattle straying over the cliffs or down to inland creeks, as Gabriel Oak's sheep did in Hardy's *Far from the Madding Crowd*.

So there are more hedges here than elsewhere; and they vary enormously—from dry-stone walls, with rough blocks of granite the size of a bullock, to wild thickets where black and white thorn, privet and yew, holly and ivy, briar and sweet-briar, bramble and briony fight each other for the light, growing ever taller and taller, so that the narrow lanes become tunnels, and field is divided from field by a barrier which stops men as well as cattle. It is not very often that one sees straying cattle in Cornwall, unless someone has carelessly left a gate open. Sometimes, indeed, one may be startled by a cow's face peering through the hedge at one, or a sheep's, or a lamb's.

One of my favourite stories about a Cornish hedge concerns the great actor Henry Irving, who was brought up in the country near Truro by an aunt. When he was ten or 11, he went through a somewhat lachrymose religious phase (nonconformism would have been rampant in the area at that time); and when, on a country walk, he saw a little lamb peering at him from the top of a hedge, he thought of it immediately as a symbol of innocence, joy and love. Painfully, wetly, with infinite difficulty, he climbed the hedge, brambles tearing his clothes and his flesh. At length he reached the top, threw his arms round the lamb's neck, and kissed it.

The lamb bit him.

But that is perhaps beside the point, which is that the high hedges of the county are uniquely beautiful; and the stone hedges of the moorlands, if not as beautiful, are even more interesting, for they must (many of them) be as old as the *fogous* and quoits they surround. W. H. Hudson tells how, in the early years of the century, he spent a whole day following one such hedge, 'beginning among the masses of granite on the edge of the cliff, and winding away inland to lose itself eventually among the rocks and gullies and furze thickets at the foot of a great boulder-strewn hill.... [It] resembled the huge prehistoric walls or earthworks made of chalk on the downs in Southern England, which meander in an extraordinary way. It was also larger than the other hedges, which crossed its winding course at all angles, being in most parts six to seven feet high, and exceedingly broad; moreover, where the stones could be seen they appeared to be more closely fitted together than in other hedges.'

It is sometimes possible to use such hedges as footpaths, and to walk along the tops of them (as one would walk along Hadrian's Wall) more safely and readily than on the ground.

But to return to Morvah, and the coastal path : one can only follow the road to Zennor, perhaps making the detour out to the end of Gurnards Head, halfway between Zennor and Porthmeor, for the sake of yet another remarkable view.

Zennor is hardly even a village: the Church, and the Tinner's Arms pub, opposite it (where, only 25 years ago, I was served a *tumbler* of very good sherry for a shilling; they don't drink much sherry round Zennor way). The nave of the Church (of St. Sennor, a totally unknown and untraceable Celtic saint, and no relation to St. Senan of Scattery) is Norman; but not outstanding, except for one of its two bench-ends, which has a carving of a mermaid—the mermaid of Zennor, commemorated in several legends and an excellent poem by John Heath-Stubbs.

The dedication of the Church reminds me that the list of saints to whom Cornish Churches are dedicated is an endless delight and amusement, and a torment to anyone who might think of discovering much more about them than their simple names. Saints Adwena and Nonna, Petroc and Rumonus, Budock and Breaca, Uny, Gocianus and Meubred ... each with his or her own feast day, and sometimes with superstitions and legends ready attached. Occasionally, in the handwritten or typed Church histories to be found near the poor box, one can find an attempt at explanation: I remember a note evidently first written by some Victorian Vicar, and carefully preserved in one Church. In faded but dogged handwriting, it announced that 'Nothing is known of our patron saint except that she may have come from Babylonia'.

It was near Zennor that D. H. Lawrence and his wife lived for a while at the beginning of the First World War, sharing a house with the Middleton Murrys in an atmosphere of tearing rows which must have disturbed the peace of the area to no small extent. I have met one or two farmers who remember Lawrence: 'Neat little, quick little, foxy little red-haired man', one of them said; 'but nice with it'. Nice is not precisely the word one associates with the Lawrences, and the Cornish eventually hounded them out. Frieda Lawrence was of course German, which might have started rumours that their uncommunicativeness strengthened. Anyway, they were suspected of being spies. Frieda was said to spend her time signalling with lights to passing U-boats, the couple were visited by the police, and virtually thrown out of their house within 24 hours. Despite which, Lawrence loved the Cornish: they were, he wrote in a letter, 'most, most unwarlike, soft, peaceable, ancient. No men could suffer more than they, at being conscripted—at any rate those that

6   *Truro Cathedral and the north aisle of St. Mary's Church*

were with me. Yet they accepted it all: they accepted it, as one of them said to me, with wonderful purity of spirit—I could howl my eyes out over him—because they "believed first of all in their duty to their fellow man".'

The Lawrences, and the Middleton Murrys, and Peter Warlock the composer, all of them loved the Land's End peninsula. Lawrence described it vividly:

'I have never seen anything so beautiful as the gorse this year, and the blackthorn. The gorse blazes in sheets of yellow fire, and the blackthorn is like white smoke, filling the valley bed. Primroses and violets are full out, and the bluebells are just coming. It is very magnificent and royal. The sun is just sinking in a flood of gold. One would not be astonished to see the cherubim flashing their wings and coming towards us, from the west....'

From Zennor to St. Ives, the coastal footpath strikes off on its own again, pleasantly remote from main road traffic. But all too soon, one is striking down Burthallan Lane, or past Clodgy Point and along the top of Porthmeor Beach, and into St. Ives itself. All too soon? Yes, alas.

Although people who knew St. Ives before the War will still have a soft spot for it, and until the end of the 'fifties it was still bearable, now the hippies against whom the local council inveighs, tousled and long-haired, decorative and dirty and on the whole mild, are almost the least offensive thing about the town. Like the other Cornish show-places, it is jammed with tourists in the season, so that driving anywhere near it becomes a torture, and trying to get a meal in comfort, almost impossible.

This is the price St. Ives has paid for concentrating on the tourist trade—which, indeed, it had to, or die. Cornwall still has the highest unemployment rate in the country, and apart from the china clay industry, farther east, there is nothing here for young men to do. Let me not detract from St. Ives' qualities as a holiday centre: it remains picturesque, if crowded; it has two very fine beaches, where the bathing is as safe as anywhere in the county; its hotels and boarding-houses, stretching along the cliff to Carbis Bay, give a good service.

If one ignores the modern buildings which pock the area like cardboard boxes in a rockery, one can still see the plan of the original

7 *Portloe, between Falmouth and Mevagissey*

fishing village which lay undisturbed until the turn of the century—
if 'plan' is not too strong a word. Nothing could be further, in fact,
from anyone's idea of a 'planned' town; and as one walks through
it, one can guess why, for every now and and again outcrops of rock
burst through to make a sudden step necessary, or bulge the side of
a house. The first settlers built their houses where they could: where
a flat rock surface offered itself. The late-comers had to make do
with the best foundations available, and if these happened to be set
at a 47° angle from the house next door, so be it.

The result is a town which can be explored for many days without allowing one to feel one has exhausted the possibilities: a sudden alley leads from street to square to quayside by a circuitous
route which from the air might seem inevitable, but at ground level
seems quite extraordinarily obtuse. Anyone whose sense of direction
is less than perfect will need the whole of his holiday if he is to feel,
when he leaves, that he 'knows' St. Ives.

Fish Street and Salubrious Place, Umfula Place, Gabriel Street and
The Stennack, have a habit of appearing on one's left, and then
again a few minutes later on one's right, or dead ahead—a habit
shared by other Cornish streets in other Cornish towns. Architecturally (again, like most other Cornish towns) St. Ives is undistinguished: possibly the best thing in the fifteenth-century Church is the
Madonna and Child by the contemporary sculptor Barbara Hep-
worth, who for many years has made her home and her studio here.
Up on the hill above the town Tregenna Castle (1774) might once
have been interesting; but has been distorted and rearranged by
British Rail (or the old G.W.R., which first acquired it as an hotel).

Apart from these, the only 'architectural' note of any originality
is struck by the Knill Monument, put up on a hill overlooking the
town in 1782 by John Knill, mayor and smuggler, for reasons of his
own. He stipulated that every five years ten virgins of ten years old
should dance round it. They still do, although they are now officially
described as 'maidens'.

On Feast Monday, in February, St. Ives holds its hurling: a game
more or less vicious in character, and played between two teams of
men, one theoretically from 'uplong' and one from 'downlong'.
St. Ives will tell you to an inch where uplong ends and downlong
begins, just as it will know the rules of hurling. No one is likely to

be able, however, to explain adequately either the rules of the game or the geographical choice of teams. Daniel Defoe had the last word about hurling: 'I confess I see nothing in it, but that it is a rude, violent play among the boors or country people; brutish and furious, and a sort of an evidence that they were once a kind of barbarians.'

Undoubtedly, on a summer's evening, St. Ives is a pleasant place to be, in some ways despite the crowds, in some ways because of them. Along the quay built by Smeaton, who built the Eddystone light, and designed several West Country harbours, one can stroll as the sun goes down, and on a Sunday evening listen to the distant sound of hymns from the nonconformist chapels, or to the band of the Salvation Army on the harbourside. Nonconformism is still strong in Cornwall, though people tend to transfer from Chapel to Church for weddings and funerals; and there are still some wonderfully original local preachers, though perhaps few likely to give out the exasperated complaint of one old man of 30 years ago. A drought had ended, and the wind and rain were beating on the chapel roof, and beating down (he knew) the crops also.

'O Lord', he prayed, 'truly we have had a long, dry old spell of it, and constantly have we offered petitions for rain for the cisterns and crops; but, O Lord, *this is ridiculous.*' At least one Vicar of St. Ives had an equally pungent sense of the ridiculous: he told the diarist Francis Kilvert that the smell of fish from St. Ives quay could be strong enough to stop the church clock.

It is on the quay at St. Ives that one may first become fully aware of the seagulls of Cornwall. Of course, they will have been wheeling and dealing around the cliffs of Land's End, and will have found you even at the *fogou* of Sancreed (especially if you have been picnicking: my mother once had a saffron bun—another peculiarly Cornish delicacy—seized from her very hand by an impertinent blackheaded gull, while she was looking the other way). But at St. Ives, as if unconscious of the fact that the fishing industry has diminished almost to nothing, so that the quayside is no longer awash with fish-heads and innards, they really crowd around, reminding one uneasily of Hitchcock's film *The Birds* (perhaps Daphne du Maurier got the idea for the original novella from watching the gulls at Fowey?) But these gulls are friendly souls, and their aerobatics in pursuit of thrown buns and biscuits are worth encouragement.

Even someone who knows nothing about birds can easily see five different species of gulls drifting and diving over a Cornish harbour in an afternoon's sun: the herring gull and the lesser black-backed gull are most common, with one or two great blackbacks keeping them in order. Then, the smallest of the crowd, the common and blackheaded gulls, forced to the outside of any scramble for food by the sheer physical weight and numbers of the others.

The Cornishman may complain at the noise and veracity of the gulls, but he still cherishes a strange almost superstitious regard for them; the gull seems, like the albatross, to have some unassailable place in Cornish mythology. I suppose that one's affection for them might have its origin not so much in superstition as in the fact that a large haul of fish would mean a vociferous welcome for the homecoming fishermen—and would also mean a safe return, not by any means invariable in these tricky waters. So the sound of gulls was a double sign of a happy day. There is also, of course, the traditional story that the gull embodies the soul of a dead fisherman: anyone who wants to see the power of that belief set forth visibly has only to look at the wonderful, naïve paintings of the fisherman Alfred Wallis.

At any event, the gull is a part of the Cornish scene to an extent unrivalled by any other bird anywhere else in the British Isles; like the sound of the sea, the wild shriek of his voice is heard everywhere —he follows the ploughman as he follows the seaman. If there are no longer such vast whirlwinds, tornados of gulls as there were when the fishing industry was at its height, the gull is still likely to dominate the memory (and the ciné-film) of any visitor.

The atmosphere of St. Ives remains much as it has been for centuries (*pace* the tourists). The artists' colony has altered things remarkably little, on the whole, although there have been the equivalent of 'town-and-gown' disputes from time to time since Whistler and Sickert 'discovered' the town in the 1880s, and brought their friends to experience the bright light of the western land. In a former chapel in Norway Square the St. Ives Society of Artists holds its exhibitions—of paintings for the most part traditional and photographic; in Back Road West the Penwith Society has its more experimental shows, with abstract paintings and carvings. There was a very loud dispute between traditionalists and avant-gardistes just after the War, and the artistic community split down the middle with a splintering noise which still occasionally echoes. But there are good and interesting paintings to be found in both galleries, and at lower prices than either *genre* would command in the West End.

The people of St. Ives are very self-contained, and although they are as caught up in the twentieth century (thanks to the media) as the people of any similar community in the country, they retain something of that canniness and sharpness of wit which their ancestors had. The best introduction to them—and, still, the best account anywhere of Cornish village life—can be found in the novels of 'Q', or Sir Arthur Quiller Couch, a much undervalued critic and minor novelist, and the most considerable Cornish writer of his time. Particularly in *Nicky-Nan, Reservist* (set in Polperro, where his grandfather lived), but also in *Troy Town* and his other novels of Cornish life, he paints the most insighted picture of the Cornishman at home; and in essentials the picture is still recognisable.

CHAPTER TWO

From Penzance
to Falmouth

It is a short bus-ride from St. Ives to Penzance, through Lelant (in the church is a beautiful memorial to William Praed, who died in 1620, and his family, with kneeling figures, flowers, a sand-glass and skull), and under the shadow of Trencrom, a hill which stands out against the sky so that one can quite clearly see even from a distance that at its height was once a fortified encampment. It is from the St. Ives-Penzance road, after it has joined the A30—a road which ends only when England ends—that one has one's first view of Mount's Bay, and St. Michael's Mount itself: 'the great vision of the guarded mount' that Milton saw. But first, Penzance.

I lived and worked here for five years, and enjoyed it very much; but I must confess that it is really a rather dull town. Its one main street, mounting steadily from the station to the nineteenth-century Market House, with its impressive Ionic portico, is attractive; there are one or two nice Georgian houses; a beautiful semi-tropical garden with a private library founded in 1818; a regency terrace facing the sea, which is still much as it must have been when it was built— though on the whole the Promenade is a failure, patched on to give a grand effect to what is essentially a small town.

Much of Penzance, indeed, is spoiled: Market Jew Street is fast losing its character, and there has been a great deal of destruction. It is fair to say that the spoliation is by no means all modern: perhaps the reason why Penzance as a whole lacks architectural identity is that the Spaniards burned down every notable building in the place in 1595; otherwise there might at least have been a nucleus to shape the town round. It was rebuilt, but as with London after the Great Fire, any budding ideas of giving it a real 'shape' were trodden down. The effect can still be seen.

46

One piece of history perhaps worth recalling is that the Brontës have a connection with Penzance: and if one looks at the well-known portrait of his three sisters by Branwell Brontë (and indeed at his own portrait and character) it is not difficult to see a certain Cornishness about the features. Their mother was a Miss Maria Branwell, the daughter of a Penzance merchant—'not pretty, but very elegant', Mrs. Gaskell says, 'and always dressed with a quiet simplicity of taste, which accorded well with her general character, and of which some of the details call to mind the style of dress preferred by her daughter [Charlotte] for her favourite heroines'. After Mrs. Brontë's early death, her elder sister arrived in Yorkshire to look after the family, and by all accounts never ceased to compare the northern landscape unfavourably with the mild south-west. Perhaps she said enough to set the whole Brontë family against Cornwall for life; there are no references to the county in the novels, at all accounts!

But the most notable of Penzance's citizens was undoubtedly Sir Humphry Davy, whose statue stands looking eastward from the Market House, out over a public lavatory and the length of Market Jew Street. The son of a wood-carver, he learned French in his youth from refugees living in West Cornwall (a mark of liveliness and opportunism); and when his mother took James Watts' son as a lodger, thus unwittingly putting Humphry in touch with the greatest scientific minds of his time, it was very soon clear what bent his mind was to follow. Thomas Beddoes, an eccentric doctor, put young Davy in charge of his Bristol laboratory, where he investigated the properties of nitrous oxide, and through his experiments discovered 'laughing gas', sodium, and potassium. He went to London in his early twenties, to be welcomed by the Royal Society, to whom he gave a discourse remarkable for its adult restraint and wisdom.

'Science', he said, 'has bestowed on man powers which may be almost called creative; which have enabled him to modify and change the beings surrounding him, and by his experiments to interrogate nature with power, not simply as a scholar, passive and seeking only to understand her operations, but rather as a master, active with his own instruments.'

The invention of the miners' safety lamp is now the main reason for his immortality: he clasps it firmly as he looks solemnly from the Market House portico out to the Mount, and one remembers Coleridge's description of his lively mind: 'living thoughts spring up like turf under his feet.'

The parish church of Penzance, St. Mary's, is nineteenth century, and scarcely more interesting than the Baptist Chapel of more or less the same period; just up the street—Chapel Street!—from both is a painstaking, not to say breathtaking, replica of the former Robinson's Egyptian Hall in Piccadilly. The Regent Hotel, almost opposite, and the Union, nearby, are both good buildings; in the courtyard of the Union are the remains of a singular Georgian theatre, now a garage: it is like the rescued Georgian theatre at Richmond in Yorkshire, and could itself probably still be rescued. But the Cornish are not great lovers of architecture, or even of history, and this does not seem likely. The hotel boasts a beautiful dining-room, from the balcony of which (when it was an assembly room) the Mayor of the time became the first Englishman to announce news of the battle of Trafalgar and the death of Nelson; a Penzance fishing boat had met the battered *Victory* returning home with the commander's body in its butt of rum.

What else is there to say of Penzance? Truly, not much. A clearing-house for the early vegetables and flowers from the Isles of Scilly and from western growers; the railway-head from which Newlyn fish are sent up-country; the starting point from which to explore the surrounding countryside. That is all.

I have perhaps spent too much time on this corner of Cornwall: but of all this unique county, it is perhaps the most unique area. Other parts of the county could be mistaken, at a pinch, for parts of Devon—Bodmin Moor and Exmoor, for instance, are superficially much alike. But West Cornwall, never. Before we quite move away, however, I ought to mention the first of the notable Cornish gardens: Trengwainton, two miles west of Penzance off the A3071. The garden is long and narrow, part of it divided by walls into a series of smaller plots with Australasian and other tropical and subtropical plants. By a stream which runs parallel with the drive are beautiful waterside plants (the Asiatic primulas are particularly splendid), and elsewhere one can stroll on grass paths through well-established rhododendron and magnolia bushes—over 20 different kinds of them. Huge banks of hydrangeas colour the late summer.

From my bedroom window in a Penzance attic 20 years ago, I could look down over a raft of rooftops to Mount's Bay, into which 350 years earlier Spenser and Raleigh had sailed on their return from Ireland:

> *There did a loftie mount at first vs greet*
> *Which did a stately heape of stones vpreare,*
> *That seemd amid the surges for to fleet*
> *Much greater than that frame, which vs did beare:*
> *There did our ship her fruitfull wombe vnlade ...*

My view was almost exactly that recorded by the young genius John Opie, in a painting which hangs in Lord St. Levan's drawing-room in the castle which sits astride the top of St. Michael's Mount —the castle, according to legend, which housed the giant disposed of by Jack. The fairy story, an echo of other tales recorded in Scandinavian legend, took root in the English consciousness, and was firmly set in the Cornish landscape—as James Orchard Halliwell recorded in his famous 1894 book of *Popular Rhymes and Nursery Tales*:

'In those days the Mount of Cornwall was kept by a huge and monstrous giant of eighteen feet in height, and about three yards in compass, of a fierce and grim countenance, the terror of all the neighbouring towns and villages....'

He was not the last (though perhaps the largest) of his race: several unusually large skeletons have been dug up in various parts of Cornwall, and there was of course the Cornish 'giant' Anthony Payne, who was born at Stratton, in the Tamar valley, at the beginning of the seventeenth century, and who was eight feet tall by the time he was 21. Anthony was the son of a tenant of Sir Bevil Grenville of Stowe, and engaged as a servant was obviously a handy young man to have about the place. He could easily carry a deer home across his shoulders, and sent out one Christmas to look for a tardy ass bearing firewood, reappeared with the ass and its load across his back.

When Sir Bevil took the royalist side during the civil war, Payne became his personal bodyguard, and fought at the battle of Stamford Hill, where he was seen a day later helping to bury the dead, whistling cheerfully, a corpse under each arm. That same year, Sir Bevil died at the battle of Lansdown, in Somerset; and Payne brought his body home to Stowe. He went to Plymouth with his old master's son, John, who was appointed Governor of the Garrison; and it was there King Charles I encountered him, made him Halberdier of the Guns, and commissioned Sir Godfrey Kneller to paint his portrait as he stood proudly holding his halberd, and with his right hand on the breach of a cannon. (The picture is at Truro Museum.)

But to return to the seat of the first and original giant, St. Michael's Mount is the home of Christian myth as well as fairy tale. Its history as a holy place began with a visit of St. Keyne and her nephew Caradoc, in the sixth century. St. Keyne was associated with South Wales and Western Herefordshire, as well as with Cornwall; Southey wrote a comic poem about her well, near Liskeard; and she appeared at Brecknock as well as at the Mount. And that is about all anyone knows about St. Keyne. A century after her visit, William of Worcester reported the appearance of St. Michael on the highest rock of the place; a Celtic monastery was set up there, and granted by Edward the Confessor to the abbey of Mont-Saint-Michel, in Normandy.

A few Celtic monks probably remained on guard until the end of the eleventh century (nothing has survived of their cells); but the Norman abbey then sent its builders to construct a monastery for a prior and 12 Benedictines, blessed by the Abbot Bernard and sent to the miniature replica of the Norman Mount to pray over the unregenerate Cornish. The walls of the Chevy Chase room in the present castle may perhaps be part of the original abbey, for that room was certainly on the site of the refectory. But otherwise nothing remains of the early buildings except a rock chamber below the choir of the chapel—which might as well be the cave of the giant Cormoran as anything else.

The religious community was suppressed in 1425—by which time it had been realised that whatever the value of the Mount might be to it, its value as a military stronghold was undoubtedly greater to the nation. The little harbour became one of the busiest in Cornwall, and with money raised by dues claimed from all the ships that used it, it was strengthened and enlarged until it provided shelter and protection for many ships. The Mount itself became a fortress: Henry de Pomeroi held it for King John while Richard I was in captivity;

during the Wars of the Roses, fugitives from the Battle of Barnet disguised themselves as pilgrims visiting the shrine (administered by the Brigittine nuns of Syon, to whom Henry vi had given it)—and the Sheriff of Cornwall, Sir John Arundell, was killed trying to throw them out. They held the Mount until an official pardon reached them.

In 1497, Perkin Warbeck chose the rough dwelling at the very top of the Mount as the safest place to leave his wife when he marched up-county to Bodmin to proclaim himself Richard iv. After his defeat, Henry sent to the Mount for her (accounts marking down £20 for her food as she rode from Cornwall to London are still in existence). Struck by her beauty, he pardoned her, and she lived to marry a knight and die in her bed.

At the time of the dissolution of the monasteries, the shrine at the Mount was served only by an archpriest and two chaplains, with an income from Syon of only £33 6s. 8d. a year (though one would like to know to what extent the first archpriest, William Morton, received payment for his assiduity in building up the Mount's defences). When the priests were finally sent packing we do not know; nor have historians traced what happened to the treasures of the shrine, which were very rich indeed—an image of St. Michael in silver-gilt, with clothes of cloth of gold and a gold chain with thick jewels; five silver ships, 43 silver rings, a silver plate; Henry vi's sword and spurs, and a silver and gilt shrine containing the jaw-bone of St. Apollyen; pyxes and chalices and monstrances, copes and albs and coin besides.... Now, alas, all that remains are a sixteenth-century chalice and seven foreign candlesticks!

The Mount has always retained a religious air: when Elizabeth's government sold it to raise money for her wars, a priest had to be maintained, along with the soldiers to defend the island. But the monastery was decaying: Leland found only a few buildings there in the 1530s, and none of these survive. The emphasis was shifting to defence already, and by the middle of the sixteenth century 'the place of the Mount is a stronghold and a whole defence for the Mount's Bay which is a great harbour and loading for ships. And this hold of the mount is requisite to be furnished with gunners, for it is the only safeguard and defence of the whole country in these parts.'

That it was not, nevertheless, impregnable became clear to a small group of Cornishmen fighting to retain the use of the Latin mass during the Prayer Book Rebellion of 1549. At low tide their opponents took the foot of the castle, sent up a smoke-screen by lighting trusses of hay 'to clench the defendents' sight and dead their shot', and the Mount was surrendered after a skirmish during which nobody was killed, 'rather by God's gracious providence than any want of will', Carew says.

Perhaps the Government felt that a heavily armed Mount provided a too-secure refuge for rebels, for the fortifications were allowed to crumble away: by 1642 the gun-platforms were rotten and the guns useless. As the Civil War began to stir, repairs were hurriedly carried out: soon the Mount became again a fortress, and once more a refuge for women-folk. It was at her home on the Mount that the wife of Francis Bassett received his almost hysterical letter of May 18, 1643, letting her know of the brilliant Royal victory at Stratton:

'Dearest Soule, Oh Deare Soule, prayse God everlastingly. Reede ye inclosed. Ring out yor Bells. Rayse Bonefyers, publish these Joyfull Tydings, Beleeve these Truthes. Excuse my writing larger. I have not tyme. We march on to meete our Victoryous ffrinds, and to sease all ye Rebells left if we can ffinde such Lyvinge....'

Bassett had been appointed Governor of the Mount in 1644 by the King, 'to kill and slay all such as shall rebelliously and trayterously disturbe the Peace ... and by the best Wayes and meanes you can to keepe and preserue itt for our service'. It had been he who had repaired the defences, at his own cost: two new gun platforms on the quay, and two more 'in Widow Browne's cellar' [sic]; two more on the seaward side of the castle. He put up a new embattled gate leading from the quay to the causeway, and for £17 erected again the platform at the west side of the castle, high above the bay, where some of his small cannon still point towards Long Rock and Penzance. He spent over £1,620 on the fortifications, over some years (full details of his expenses are preserved). It was a generous sum, for he also spent a great deal of money elsewhere in the cause of the King; so it is not surprising that his brother, succeeding to command of the Mount after Bassett's death, was hard pressed for funds. He was disappointed in his expectations of some financial help from Royalist sources.

Disillusioned by the thanklessness of the king's friends, and fully aware that any real damage to the Mount and its castle would completely ruin him, Sir Arthur Bassett surrendered it to the Parliamentarians the moment it came under threat; by this time, the Cornishmen in the garrison and the countryside around were equally weary, and also capitulated. A few years later, Bassett sold the Mount to Col. John Aubyn, an ancestor of the Lord St. Levan, who still lives there.

The castle's interior is not spectacularly beautiful, though the Chevy Chase Room (renamed after a seventeenth-century plaster frieze showing—among other sports—ostrich-hunting!) is pretty, and the drawing-rooms which an eighteenth-century St. Aubyn remodelled from the old lady chapel are delightful, and contain not only the Opie landscape, but a good Gainsborough.

Opie, by the way, was the most striking artist Cornwall has yet produced. He was the son of a carpenter and builder who worked in St. Agnes, and seems instinctively to have taken to drawing and painting portraits from the moment he could master a brush. When he was still in his teens he sold a portrait for five shillings, and came running home shouting: 'I'm set up for life!' 'That boy', remarked his father, 'will come to hanging.'

After a few years' travelling from farmhouse to farmhouse painting anyone who would pay a small fee (some of the early, naïve portraits are a charming record of eighteenth-century domestic life), he was befriended by John Walcot, a doctor practising in Truro. Walcot himself was a character: he had begun life as a physician with William Trelawny, Governor of Jamaica; then he took holy orders; but returned to Cornwall, whence he went, accompanied by Opie, to London.

There, as Peter Pindar, Opie became well known as a satirist, publishing a series of pungent attacks on George III (showing the king being taken on a solemn state tour of Whitbread's breweries, and musing simply on the philosophical problem of how apples got into dumplings). Opie, meanwhile, established himself as a fashionable portraitist; hung at the Royal Academy (his father's prophecy fulfilled?) he painted over 500 portraits, and became known as a wit. Mrs. Siddons, the famous actress, used to say: 'I like to meet Mr. Opie, for then I always hear something I did not know before.' And in his *Conversations*, James Northcote leaves many sketches of Opie's character: 'I do not say he was always right, but he always put your thoughts into a new track that was worth following. I was very fond of Opie's conversations, and I remember once when I was expressing my surprise at his having so little of the Cornish dialect, "Why", he said, "the reason is, I never spoke at all till I knew you and Walcott!" He was a true genius.'

Opie died in a fashionable house in Berners Street, Professor of Painting at the Academy. He and Walcot lie near each other in the crypt of St. Paul's.

It is the whole ambience of St. Michael's Mount and its castle, as Opie saw, which makes it one of the real delights of west Cornwall. Below the living-room in the south-east wing, for instance—built with fairly restrained Gothic taste in 1876—three bedroom floors tumble down the precipitous side of the rock face, looking towards the sea. It is a startling, wholly attractive effect. The north-west wing is as late as 1927; but a miracle of good taste occurred—the building holds together marvellously well.

The road from Penzance which passes through Marazion, at the foot of the Mount, sweeps on, never more than a stone's-throw from the sea, to Helston and the Lizard peninsula. The Lizard is the southernmost point of Britain, as Land's End is the westernmost; it seems sometime to be made wholly of serpentine—veins of dark green, brown and red, running through the rock at Kynance Cove, and sparkling in the sun. Some giant might have been working in mosaic on a clumsily large scale; and he also presumably built the church at Ruan Minor, with its serpentine tower.

Clinging to the cliffs, one can occasionally see the whitish flowers of the samphire, which Edgar leading the blind Lear pretended to see at Dover:

> *Halfway down*
> *Hangs one that gathers samphire—dreadful trade.*

Only a century ago, the poorest Cornish families were still forced to clamber perilously over these cliffs to pick samphire to sell as a relish, at market. A man and wife, their four children left at home, fell to their deaths at the end of the last century.

It is the physical line of the country which is most attractive at the Lizard: the villages are 'quaint' enough, if quaintness still attracts. But though they are worth seeing, they are not perhaps worth going to see. One might remember Porthleven as the village where Henry Trengrouse (a Helston cabinet-maker) tried out his rocket-firing life-saving apparatus, which after much persuasion he finally persuaded lifesavers to use; it preserved over 10,000 lives between 1870 and 1920 alone.

But what I remember—no doubt improperly—with more continual interest and amusement is the visit to the Lizard in 1860 by Tennyson and Palgrave: it was in fact at the Lizard that Palgrave planned his famous *Golden Treasury*, the anthology that above all others formed poetic taste for a generation.

Tennyson had had plans for his great Arthurian poems jostling about in his brain for some years, already; and no doubt was after atmosphere. With him to Cornwall travelled Palgrave and three other friends—Holman Hunt, Val Prinsep, and Thomas Woolner. At first, all was well—though the Cornish evidently found the party somewhat odd (one evening, after listening to their conversation, an old gentleman approached them and said: 'Of all the extraordinary men I have ever heard, your party are the most extraordinary. Pray tell me your names.' Tennyson was introduced as 'Mr. Poelaur'; Palgrave tactlessly referred to him as 'the old gentleman'.

But after a few halycon days diving off rocks into the deep blue breakers, and visiting briefly the Scilly Isles, the peaceful interlude began to break up. Palgrave had been asked by Mrs. Tennyson to 'keep an eye on Alfred', and wherever the Laureate went he was followed by an insistent figure everlastingly bleating 'Tennyson! Tennyson!' Finally, the poet announced that he had had enough; he was going. Early next morning he jumped into a pony trap and made for Penzance—but not before Palgrave, at the last moment, had rushed from the Inn to jump up beside him. The pair drove off, their vehement arguing voices dying on the clean morning air.

Mawgan-in-Meneage, St. Martin-in-Meneage, Landewednack, Grade and Mullion are of pleasant passing interest; even Helston, with its broad Coinagehall-street, water running through open conduits at each side, and threatening to spill into the very hallway of the Angel

Inn (once the town house of the great Godolphins) is notable less for itself than for an Event. The Event is, of course, the Helston Flora Dance, danced to

> *the band with the curious tone*
> *Of cornet, clarinet and big trombone.*

But one feels guilty at quoting the words of that favourite Edwardian baritone solo, for it typifies the way in which the Helston furry-dance has become a 'foreign' event, directed at the tourist industry, and the film and television cameras. At Padstow, the annual hobby-horse celebrations retain something of their original, ancient, strange mystery; at Helston, all is peculiarly artificial, now, and even at the popular afternoon dance the streets are awash with people who barely know the steps of the dance, and have even less notion of what it was originally all about.

Even the name is wrong: not long before the turn of the century, the original name—the Furry Dance—was commonly used; few people call it that today. The Furry (in Middle English, *ferier*) was simply a 'parish feasten holiday', and in Helston's case was held at the festival of St. Michael and Archangel, patron saint of the town and Church, and famed for his aerial battle with the Devil, a few hundred feet above the quaking town. But in fact the dance undoubtedly pre-dates Christianity.

Through the streets at dawn in the most ancient times came the Hal-an-Tow procession, men and girls with flowers and oak twigs in their hair, led by an old woman on a donkey, while the church bells rang out a welcome:

> *With Hal-an-Tow, Rum-ble, O! for we were up*
> *as soon as any day, O!*
> *And for to fetch the summer home, the summer and*
> *the May, O!*
> *For summer is a-come, O! and winter is a-gone, O!*

It is the noon dance which has mainly survived: led by the Mayor with his beadles, and the town band, the dancers go through the town, in at the front door of a house and out at the back, top hats glittering (for this one day of the year) in the sun—or, rather more often, glistening softly under a midday drizzle. This dance re-

8   *St. Austell Bay from the Little Gribbin; Polkerris in the centre*

mains 'for the gentry'—or at all events for invited dancers. There is a children's dance in the morning, and a free-for-all in the afternoon. It remains great fun, although the crowds, the cars, and the litter make it less enjoyable than it was even a quarter of a century ago.

In parenthesis, anyone who is interested to read a splendidly accurate picture of Helston in the eighteenth century could do no better than unearth a copy of the three novels making up the Penhale trilogy, written between the wars by Crosbie Garstin.

To the north of Helston, lie Camborne and Redruth—or, rather, lies Camborne-Redruth, for the two towns, no-nonsense industrial communities, are more or less one. They throve, years ago, as the centre of the Cornish mining industry. They are no longer that, though the Camborne School of Mines, founded 80 years ago, remains an important centre of education in the techniques of metalliferous mining.

Outside the Free Library at Camborne is a bust of Richard Trevithick, the inventor of the high-pressure steam engine. The son of a mine-manager, he barely learned to read and write at school, where he was reported as 'disobedient, slow, obstinate, spoiled ... frequently absent and very inattentive'. He invented his engine in 1800, when he was almost 30, in response to the general dissatisfaction with Watts' steam engines, which were not only forced to remain stationary, but were also expensive. In 1801, Davies Gilbert watched as one of the earliest engines juddered and hissed its way on to the roads.

'The Travelling Engine took its departure from Camborne Church Town for Tehidy on 28 December, where I was waiting to receive it. The carriage, however, broke down after travelling very well and up an ascent, in all about three or four hundred yards. The carriage was forced under some shelter, and the Parties adjourned to the Hotel, and comforted their hearts with a Roast Goose and proper drinks; when, forgetful of the Engine, its water boiled away, the Iron became red hot, and nothing that was combustible remained either of the Engine or the House.'

Three years later, Trevithick installed one of his engines at Greenwich; it blew up almost immediately. Trevithick noted, in a style informed by his years of inattention at school: 'it killed 3 on the spot and one other is sense dead of his wounds.... I believe

9 *Bodmin Moor near Rough Tor*

that Mr. B and Watt is abt to do mee every enjurey in their power for they have don their outemost to repoart the exploseion both in the newspapers and private letters very different to what it really is....'

But he persevered, and in 1804 built a tramway locomotive which drove nine miles in just over four hours; later he took his engines to Peru and became involved in the Peruvian Civil War, inventing a carbine for use there. In 1833, he died a pauper, and was buried in an unmarked grave. But at Camborne, neat in swallow-tailed coat, he stares solemnly up Beacon Hill, up which his 'puffing devil' carried 12 passengers at slightly under a walking pace, in 1801. And as they pass, the passengers in rugby football excursion coaches commemorate the event in song:

> *Goin' up Camborne 'ill, comin' down,*
> *Goin' up Camborne 'ill, comin' down,*
> *The 'osses stood still, the wheels turned roun',*
> *Goin' up Camborne 'ill, comin' down.*

Incidentally, it was near Camborne lived that Sir William Pendarvis who, a contemporary wrote, had a coffin made of copper 'and placed it in the midst of his great hall, and instead of his making use of it as a monitor that might have made him ashamed and terrified at his past life, and induce him to make amends in future, it was filled with punch, and he and his comrades soon made themselves incapable of any sort of reflection; this was *often* repeated, and hurried him on to that awful moment he had so much reason to dread'.

But the really surprising thing about the Camborne-Redruth area, I have always thought, was the discovery in 1931 of a Roman villa at Magor, near Camborne, dating probably from the second century; yet one still reads that the Romans did not settle very much farther west than Exeter!

Falmouth must have been a tiny fishing village until the seventeenth century, though its beautiful broad bay had always been an excellent shelter for shipping, protected by Pendennis and St. Mawes castles, put up by Henry VIII. It was the Killigrew family which really developed the town: Sir Peter built its church—dedicated to King Charles the Martyr, and with its tall granite columns and long panelled roofs one of the most original and attractive, if untypical, churches in the county.

To Falmouth during the Civil War came both Prince Charles and his mother, Henrietta Maria, 'the woefullest spectacle my eyes ever let look'd on; the most worne and weake pityfull creature in the world, the poore Queene shifting for one hour's liffe longer....' Pendennis Castle, where they both stayed, was defended by its 87-year-old governor, John Arundel, for six months against the full forces of Parliament. When he finally surrendered, with one salted horse left to feed his garrison, over 200 of his men were so weak they were unable to walk—despite which Arundel was so shrewd in his bargaining that the Parliamentarians never suspected the extent of his plight.

In 1688, Falmouth was made the port from which the mail packet service sailed; this probably more than anything else brought the town great prosperity—and unwonted excitement too, for in the early years of the nineteenth century there were many battles between the packets and privateers. How the harbour must have bustled with shipping: Byron described it in one of his verse-letters to Hodgson, as he set off on Childe Harold's first journey into Europe, in 1809:

> *Now our boatman quit their mooring,*
> *And all hands must ply the oar;*
> *Baggage from the quay is lowering,*
> *We're impatient—push from shore.*
> *'Have a care! that case holds liquor—*
> *Stop the boat—I'm sick—O Lord!'*
> *'Sick ma'am, damme, you'll be sicker*
> *Ere you've been an hour on board.'*

> *Thus are screaming*
> *Men and women*
> *Gemmen, ladies, servants, Jacks;*
> *Here entangling,*
> *All are wrangling,*
> *Stuck together close as wax—*
> *Such the general noise and racket,*
> *Ere we reach the Lisbon packet.*

Byron, incidentally, also visited St. Mawes Castle, which, he wrote, was 'garrisoned by an able-bodied person of four-score, a widower. He has the whole command and sole management of six most unmanagable pieces of ordnance, admirably adapted for the destruction of Pendennis, a like tower of strength on the opposite side of the Channel.'

Now, the bay is a flutter of sails at most summer weekends; Falmouth, its importance as a port somewhat diminished, can still be what Disraeli found it: 'One of the most charming places I ever saw.'

John Wesley, whose *Journals* have a lot of say about the Cornwall of the first half of the eighteenth century, found the town less pleasant: he was besieged in a house by a mob screaming: 'Bring out the Canorum!' (a local word for Methodist). When the door was shattered, only the noble carriage and determined aspect of Wesley prevented the Cornish equivalent of a tarring-and-feathering. He eventually left: 'Many of the mob waited at the end of the town, who, seeing me escaped out of their hands, could only revenge themselves with their tongues; but a few of the fiercest ran along the shore, to receive me at my landing. I walked up the steep, narrow passage from the sea, at the top of which the foremost man stood. I, looking him in the face, said, "I wish you a good night." He spake not, nor moved hand or foot till I was on horseback. Then he said, "I wish you was in hell", and turned back to his companions.'

St. Mawes, overcrowded during the season, has an hotel where at least part of *The Wind in the Willows* was written, though the river, in that tale, is the Fowey; and nearby is St. Just in Roseland, a rather dull little church in one of the most beautiful little wooded combes it is possible to imagine. This church is one of the centres of the legend of Christ's visit to Cornwall (on the boat of Joseph of Arimathaea, said to have been interested in the tin trade, and after the Crucifixion to have been sent by the apostle Philip to be a missionary in England, where he founded the country's first Christian Church, at Glastonbury). A stone is still shown said to bear the imprint of the Saviour's foot as he stepped ashore; but I think it can be said that the story lacks evidence.

Up-river from Falmouth lies Truro, the cathedral town and administrative centre of Cornwall (though not its county town, which is Bodmin). A lovely river trip it is, past little inlets and creeks—one of them the Frenchman's Creek of Daphne du Maurier's splendid romance.

The whole area of the Fal estuary is worth exploring for its landscapes and gardens. On the road from Falmouth to the Helford River estuary, for instance, is Glendurgan, near the little village of Mawnan Smith. This garden spreads itself luxuriously over three steep valleys descending to the river, and below the house lies a walled garden with shrubs, roses, herbaceous plants and climbers. Then one can walk down to the river through drifts of bluebells, past magnificent trees, rhododendrons and drimys; and there is a pool, too, with gunneras and Asiatic primulas growing beside it. And if that were not enough, a walk of camellias, and a large and elaborate (if somewhat too easy) maze.

A mile and a half away, on the other side of Mawnan Smith, is another garden—Penjerrick, cut in two by a sunken road; the upper garden is soaked in the colours of masses of rhododendrons, azaleas, Chilean firebushes, pieris, magnolias and camellias, and the lower garden a-splash with gunneras and other water-loving plants at the side of a lake beneath the largest weeping willow, surely, in Cornwall.

Trelissick Garden (while we are on the subject) is very near the King Harry Ferry, which takes the B3289 (or at least the vehicles on it) over the narrow point at the top of Carrick Roads—the wonderfully sheltered inlet for Falmouth shipping, where on choir outings during the years immediately after the War, we peered fascinated at the rusting hulks of gunboats, and at others covered with the intricate webbing of 'mothball' protection.

The King Harry Ferry itself used to be a marvellously Emett-like machine, clawing its way along a length of chain with the help of a semi-retired steam engine. I first crossed it, as luck would have it, with Emett himself, and never quite understood why it did not become a major character in his gallery of machines. Recently, alas, it has been somewhat modernised—though it is still not for anyone in much of a hurry, and is temperamentally far more of the nineteenth than twentieth century. Not far away from it is Come-to-Good, with its charming little thatched Quaker meeting house (1709; not many thatched houses in the county). Better Come-to-Good than Hell's Mouth, on the north coast! But on to Trelissick—

The house itself is a strange neo-Greek mansion which went up in 1825, and whose portico is a spirited imitation of the Erechtheion at Athens. That must have surprised the locals. The gardens, fortunately, are under no such delusions of grandeur, and have something interesting in them besides rhododendrons (I must say I sometimes tire of the perennial Cornish rhododendron theme!). There is a great variety of shrubs, most of them flowering in spring and summer, and there are good hydrangeas too.

CHAPTER THREE

Mid-Cornwall

But now, to Truro, best entered by river, I suppose—though few tourists will have the good luck to come to it that way; most of them will arrive fuming after the long, long trail down the A390, where overtaking is as unwise as it is tempting. The town is mainly Georgian, though it is the nineteenth-century Cathedral that dominates it, the sharp twin spires darting straight to the sky, and all the more striking because Cornwall is on the whole a county of low churches with stubby towers.

These spires went up after the turn of the century, for the Cathedral was designed in 1880 (by John Loughborough Pearson), and was not finished until 1910—by the architect's son. It is not, I confess, a building much to my own taste; and I rather regret the church which Pearson pulled down to make way for it—all but its south aisle, which he incorporated into the Cathedral, and which is one of the most splendid Gothic pieces in the county. That original church, of St. Mary, must have been very fine, with its 128-foot spire. But certainly the Cathedral has a clear, unmuddled, uncluttered strength which is appealing, and its bare nave is impressively spacious.

Benson, the first Bishop of Truro, was largely responsible for raising the funds for the building of the Cathedral; he travelled by horse and trap to every corner of the county (he had to: a stronghold of methodism, Cornwall was not going to bring its money to him). And he found many strange characters among the clergy. At one Vicarage, the maid came to ask the Vicar for the key to the cellar, so that she could fetch a bottle of wine for Communion. 'Ah, yes', said the Vicar; 'we'll have white today, just for a change....' Elsewhere was a Vicar who never set foot inside his church—even as a member of the congregation—preferring to lean on his garden gate wearing a flowered dressing-gown and smoking a hookah.

Even today the tradition seems to be upheld: not so many years ago, a Vicar was missing from the church where he was supposed to be marrying a cousin of mine, and was found on the beach, cassock tucked up about his waist, paddling. The same Vicar declared a sudden and unexpected collection in the middle of another cousin's wedding, inviting the congregation in the words of a then popular song, to 'Put Another Nickle In'.

The Cathedral fails to rescue Truro (the Polchester of some of Hugh Walpole's novels) from a certain dullness, partly the result of the fact that the medieval town has almost vanished, castle and all. The local planning authority, like many elsewhere in Cornwall, has not been enormously exercised to keep any character in the town: the old Red Lion, with its 1671 frontage, and a lovely staircase, has been demolished (admittedly a runaway lorry helped in the work; but the building was already sentenced). The 1772 Assembly Rooms have gone, except for their façade. Even Lemon Street, rising up to the westward out of the town, is beginning to lose its character, though it is still beautiful.

At the top of it, one can gaze upwards at a monument which commemorates two men—Richard Lemon Lander, the explorer, who stands atop his column, and Nevil Northey Burnard, who carved him. Burnard was, like Opie, another self-taught artist (the strain is continued in the poet Jack Clemo, another extraordinary and original Cornishman).

Burnard was a stonemason's son from Altarnun, who had a penchant for carving: while he was still apprenticed to his father, he inscribed with a nail a head of Homer on a slate (now in the library of the Royal Cornwall Polytechnic Society in Falmouth), and at 15 he was fortunate enough to be sent to Place House at Fowey, to do some repairs and some original work there for Squire Treffry. He was there for two years—until 1835—and made good use of the library. A year later, he won the silver medal of the Polytechnic Society, and within a short time found himself one of the two or three most popular sculptors in England, exhibiting at the Royal Academy, and executing busts for the gentry.

But he liked drink; and this was the finish of him. He staggered back to Cornwall as a tramp, remaining a tramp shuffling from workhouse to workhouse until he died, in 1878, and was buried in a pauper's grave at Camborne, mourned only by a small band of stonemasons who happened to be working on restoration there.

Charles Causley has written of him in a memorial poem recalling his early years at Altarnun:

> *Here lived Burnard who with his finger's bone*
> *Broke syllables of light from the moorstone,*
> *Spat on the genesis of dust and clay,*
> *Rubbed with huge hands the blinded eyes of day,*
> *And through the seasons of the talking sun*
> *Walked, calm as God, the fields of Altarnun.*
>
> *The village sprawled white as a marriage bed,*
> *Gulls from the north coast stumbled overhead*
> *As Burnard, standing in the churchyard hay,*
> *Leaned on the stiff light, hacked childhood away,*
> *On the tomb slabs watched bugler, saint, dove,*
> *Under his beating fists grow big with love.*

Lander, commemorated by Burnard's statue on the column in Lemon Street, was also a really rather extraordinary man. The son of a Truro innkeeper, he went to the West Indies on a merchantman when he was only 11, and in his teens accompanied the explorer Hugh Clapperton on the latter's second South African expedition, bringing his leader's journal back to England after the latter's death at Sokoto.

The British Government sent Lander out again in 1830 to discover the course of the lower Niger; with his younger brother John he led a brilliant expedition down the river in canoes, accompanied by only a few natives, and with a simple compass as their only scientific instrument. Captured by Ibos, they were ransomed by King Boy of Brass Town, who took them to the mouth of the Niger, whence they sailed to Fernando Po, and on home with a full map of the river's course (a matter then in great dispute). Richard died in Africa in 1834, having been wounded by natives at Fernando Po, on another expedition. He was only 30. Now, I suppose, he is forgotten utterly.

Make sure of visiting the county museum and art gallery in Truro (there will certainly be a rainy day once in a fortnight to prompt it).

Although it suffers, like most provincial museums, from the old-fashioned lay-out of many rooms, it reflects the county and its life and customs remarkably well. There are many things here worth seeing, and some positively worth going to see. The fascinating pre-history of Cornwall is well represented; there is a famous collection of minerals, Roman and medieval tin ingots, and many relics of the glorious days of the mining industry (glorious, that is, for everyone but the miners). Here too is the work not only of Opie and Burnard, but of Henry Bone, one of the boys taught by Cookworthy, who started painting on Plymouth porcelain and ended by enamelling on copper. There is a splendid collection of porcelain, and among the pictures, drawings by Rowlandson and Rembrandt and Hogarth, as well as some of Opie's best paintings.

It would be idle to pretend that the countryside bounded by Truro, Newquay and St. Austell is the most interesting and beautiful in the county. But no parish in Cornwall is completely without interest (indeed, is any parish in England?) At Probus, for instance, where one of the most beautiful church towers in the district (and the tallest in the county) seems covered in a stony lace, Giles Farnaby was born, who wrote a vast number of pieces for domestic keyboard instruments, over 50 of which are in the Fitzwilliam virginal book, and who died, over 80, in 1640. He was probably the only Cornish composer of any note, though the father of Thomas Tomkins (Farnaby's contemporary) was organist for a while at Lostwithiel, before becoming Precentor of Gloucester Cathedral.

Of Newquay there is little to say except that it is a respectable modern holiday resort, with good sandy beaches, as safe as any on the north coast (which is to say, often quite dangerous). The only remotely interesting building in the town is the little white huer's hut on the headland, from which a watchman would scan the sea for shoals of pilchards. The coast road—B3276—leading north-east to Trevose Head and eventually to Padstow has some lovely views, and at Mawgan in Pydar, east of Newquay, is Lanherne, the Elizabethan mansion of the Arundell family.

John de Lanherne's daughter married an Arundell in 1231, and the family remained firmly Catholic throughout the Reformation; the sanctuary lamp in Lanherne Chapel was never extinguished—and since 1794 has burned for the Carmelite nuns who still have the house as a convent, and who attend worship concealed from other worshippers, leaving the convent only at their death. There is a secret chamber, a priest's hole, in the house, in which a priest is said to have lain concealed for 18 months during the Elizabethan period. And here, too, is the skull of the famous Cuthbert Mayne, one of the first seminary priests to land in England; Mayne often stayed at Lanherne—may indeed have used the priest's hole—'as much as a se'ennight or fortnight together'.

But at last, he was discovered—at Golden, between Truro and St. Austell; arraigned at Launceston, condemned, and after being dragged through the streets on a hurdle, torn to pieces in the usual revolting manner, and his head placed on Launceston Castle gate. What brave Catholic rescued it? At any rate, it returned to Lanherne, there one hopes to rest in peace.

On the south coast, Mevagissey is an attraction: another of the small Cornish fishing villages where on the whole the only fishing is now done in the pockets of tourists. But Mevagissey is one of the least-spoilt of the tourist traps, with its inner and outer harbours, its houses jostling each other on the hill above them. It is worth looking into the Church of St. Peter, too, for the memorial to Mr. Otwell Hill and his wife, who lie placidly side by side, an inscription declaring:

> *Stock Lancashier, Birth London, Cornwall gave*
> *To Otwell Hill Inhabitance and Grave.*
> *Frank, Frugall, Plaisannt, Sober, Stout and*
> *Kinde....*

Up a very steep hill west of Mevagissey, and on through the little hamlet of Gorran Haven, one may reach Veryan Bay, where Caerhays Castle looks out to sea over its lake. Byron's male ancestors lived here, including his grandfather, who eloped with a cousin, joined the Navy, and became an Admiral with the engaging nickname of Foulweather Jack.

St. Austell is probably the busiest and richest town in Cornwall—at the centre of the china clay industry, which provides more work than any other business in the county, and indeed turns out Britain's second largest export. The town has benefited accordingly: it has a new and moderately well-designed shopping precinct, a cinema club showing demi-semi-pornographic films, spasmodic visits from wrestlers and strippers, and a more or less floating population of shoppers with more money in their pockets than in most other Cornish towns.

It is not, on the whole, handsome, though it has a large and impressive church—Holy Trinity—which apparently once served the pre-eighteenth century village and the surrounding countryside, and must have been a sort of country cathedral.

China clay saturates the beaches of St. Austell and Par bay, from Black Head past the little port of Charlestown (one of the most charming on this coast) to Par itself. And inland, too, clay dominates the landscape, the white pyramids of waste looking from the distance like alps, and even more impressive when one drives among them, some pure white, some covered with vegetation, and below them water-filled dark pools.

It is this landscape that Jack Clemo, the blind and deaf Cornish poet, celebrates in his classic autobiography *Confession of a Rebel* (interesting that two wonderful autobiographies, that one, and A. L. Rowse's *A Cornish Childhood*, should be centred on the few square miles of country north-east of St. Austell). Clemo is one of the best landscape-poets in the country, and to read his work in the landscape itself is fascinating :

> *These white crags*
> *Cup waves that rub more greedily*
> *Now halfway up the chasm; you see*
> *Doomed foliage hung like rags;*
> *The whole clay-belly sags.*

> *What scenes far*
> *Beneath those waters: chimney-pots*
> *That used to smoke; brown rusty clots*
> *Of wheels still oozing tar;*
> *Lodge doors that rot ajar.*

> *Those iron rails*
> *Emerge like claws cut short on the dump,*

Though once they bore the wagon's thump:
Now only toads and snails
Creep round their loosened nails....

There is the flavour of this strange landscape, perfectly caught; a charmless but utterly memorable tract of land.

Not far away, on the greener uplands, at Methrose, near Luxulyan, is a beautiful early farmhouse—sixteenth century, and earlier than most comparable buildings of any size in the area. Here are granite walls, a dipping slate roof, a courtyard with a hall at its side ... and nearby, at Roche, an even more picturesque sight: a pile of rock perfectly camouflaging an ancient chapel, ruined now, but even when it was new, 500 years ago, precarious and difficult to reach.

It was licensed (as St. Michael's Chapel) in 1409, with two rooms, then—a lower one, for a chaplain or an anchorite, and the real chapel above. The task of carrying the massive granite blocks for the building up the sheer side of the rock is a feat to be wondered at. Not unnaturally, there are several legends connected with the place—one of a beautiful girl who retired there to nurse her father, who had contracted leprosy. But this seems on the whole improbable, and any pilgrimage to the rock will be rewarded more by the view than by commemorating any particular legend! All round, the clay cones shine in the sun, setting off the green of the landscape beyond.

The white sludge of clay is tacky about one's feet if one tries to bathe from Par beach, or even from the beautiful (if perilous) beach at Carlyon Bay, below the once-splendid hotel made intensely fashionable for a while during the 1930s when the Prince of Wales would sweep down and be seen beating his way around the excellent golf-course nearby.

Oddly, the clay seems to keep to the inside of the bay, so that the eastern side of the Gribbin Head is mercifully untouched, and little Polkerris is free from it. Here is one of the most charming small beaches on this coast, even at its most unbearably crowded, at weekends, when cars cram the carpark at the foot of the steep hill from the main road, and are even parked on both sides of that main road for half a mile or so each side of the turning to the village.

A tiny hamlet, with an equally tiny pier, about a dozen cottages (their white walls crowded with roses), a life-boat house now a café with good pasties and cream, and a pub with a rough platform on which one can lounge with a pint of mild, or sit on the worn barrels of the ancient guns there, Polkerris manages to retain all its individuality. Firm action against the itinerant transistor radio might help to improve it, and so might a little more action with brush and rubbish bin (the beach is, after all, privately owned, and one is charged for deckchairs or boats). But it is *wholesome*: un-quaint, with nothing plastic about it. Visit it.

The road which leads from Par to Polkerris continues to Fowey: Fowey, which looks still much as it must have looked in its great days —the days of the privateers, and later of the Civil War. Despite the truly horrific new houses which have sprung up on the hillside at Polruan, on the eastern side of the harbour, this is still one of the most beautiful towns on the coast. Twin ruined castles stand at either side of the entrance (linked by a chain in Tudor times, to close in the harbour). Place, the Treffry's house, looks like a modern attempt at a castle—and indeed, more or less is so: nineteenth century or early Victorian Gothic. But the battlements and high walls, shrouded with greenery, are charming, and with its tall towers and porphyry hall (which so charmed the visiting Victoria and Albert) it certainly bears out Prof. Pevsner's description: 'of an ambitious, somewhat elephantine Walter Scott romanticism'.

Place dominates the town, and indeed there is little elsewhere of great note even from such recent times. But there is plenty of note, all the same: the Ship Inn, for instance, once the town house of the Rashleighs, and fifteenth century; across Lostwithiel Street, a four-teenth-century house; here and there, other bits and pieces of Tudor architecture—a door here, a window there. It is the *ensemble* that matters: that and the busy harbour, and the legend of 'Troy Town' —Sir Arthur Quiller Couch's legend, for it was his book of that title which still keeps Fowey in mind. 'Q' (until A. L. Rowse, the best-known Cornish writer for a century, and now sadly undervalued both as novelist and particularly as critic) lived in a house over-looking the harbour, and used to sally through his town (he was Mayor and Commodore of the Yacht Club) in white ducks and a sailing cap. He must have felt that he *was* Fowey; and to some extent that was true.

Various factors have conspired to keep the town attractive, among them a perilously narrow main street (almost, indeed, the only street in Fowey!) which corkscrews from where the station once was to where the sea still is. I negotiated this street, not so long ago, from end to end—which is more difficult than it sounds, for I was travelling against the permitted flow of traffic. The local inhabitants found this enjoyable rather than unlawful, but I do not recommend it during the summer months. Indeed, car-drivers would do well to park outside the town, and walk down.

The Town Council has refrained from pulling down the old for the sake of erecting the new, and the result is that Fowey is still a delight, with only the gee-gaws and postcards to blemish it. Cream teas and lobster salads in sight of the sea, and the river winding up to the rival town (once the rival port) of Lostwithiel.

Kenneth Grahame spent his honeymoon at Fowey, with 'Q' and another sea-and-river-struck friend, Edward Atkinson, or 'Atky' (also sometime Commodore of the Yacht Club, and sadly drowned in a boating accident). It was at Fowey that Grahame found there was 'nothing, absolutely nothing, half so much worth doing as simply messing about in boats'. His wife, by all accounts, did not enjoy being a river widow, and the honeymoon ended in a flurry of ill-temper: but the Fowey River is immortalised, in spirit if not in name, in *The Wind in the Willows*.

Now, apart from the tourists, Fowey is quieter than it has ever been in an eventful history. The motor torpedo boats which buzzed frenetically in and out of the harbour during the Second World War, restoring a certain piratical flavour to the town, have joined the other ghosts. In the summer the flapping sails of visiting yachts or Redwings (it is not the easiest port to sail in, or out, of), or a scurry of small boats as a cumbersome china clay vessel comes bumbling out of harbour, provide the only excitement. Once more, Fowey is the Troy Town of 'Q'—

> *O the harbour of Fowey*
> *Is a beautiful spot,*
> *And it's there I enjowey*
> *To sail in a yot;*
> *Or to race in a yacht*
> *Round a mark or a buoy—*

Such a beautiful spacht
Is the harbour of Fuoy.

And as one leaves, one can look back down the hill to the harbour
—or indeed see it from the hill above Bodinnick where the 'Q' memorial stone stands—looking much as it looked 300 years ago to
Richard Carew, strolling on Hall Walk:

'In passing along, your eyes shall be called away from guiding
your feet, to descry by their farthest kenning the vast ocean sparkled
with ships that continually this way trade forth and back to most
quarters of the world. Nearer home, they take view of all sized
cocks, barges and fisherboats, hovering on the coast. Again, con-
tracting your sight to a narrower scope, it lighteth on the fair and
commodious haven, where the tide daily presenteth his double service of flowing and ebbing, to carry and recarry whatsoever the
inhabitants shall be pleased to charge him withal, and his creeks
(like a young wanton lover) fold about the land with many embracing arms....'

The road to Lostwithiel splits, a mile or two from Fowey, at the
point where the A3081 slides down to Tywardreath and Par, and the
B3269 makes on along the line of the hills. At the point where
the roads part, are crumbling lodge gates—the gates of Menabilly, the
former home of the Rashleigh family, a mansion rebuilt in the
eighteenth century, looking out over splendid early nineteenth-century landscaped gardens to the sea. If one has a *frisson* of *déjà vu*, it is
because one remembers the opening line of one of the most successful romantic novels written between the wars: 'Last night I dreamed
I went to Manderley again....' For Manderley, of Daphne du
Maurier's *Rebecca*, is Menabilly; the novelist still lives in the grounds.

On the green island outside Menabilly gates, where the three roads
meet, stands a weathered granite stone, the remains of an ancient
cross. Granite crosses are several a penny in Cornwall, but this one is
of particular interest, for beneath it may have lain the body of one
of the Western world's most romantic heroes: Tristan, whose love
for Iseult is commemorated in so many works of art from ancient
to modern times. Legend is legend; but when one examines the basis
for this one, it becomes clear that there is very strong reason to believe that the country in which the original events of the story took

10   *St. Mary Magdalen, Launceston: east porch (1511)*

place lay around this spot, and that its original narrator must have known Cornwall very well indeed.

The inscription on the Castle Dore Stone is very worn, but it is still possible to see clearly that it commemorates the son of Cunomorus, an ancient King who was also called Markus (in a ninth-century life of the sixth-century St. Paul Aurelian). The son's name has been variously read, but one credible version is Drustaus or Drustanus—an early version of Tristan.

The stone was originally found almost a mile farther along the B3269 towards Lostwithiel, at Castle Dore itself, an earth-work which stands on the very summit of the high land the road crosses. All that remains now is a blunt, overgrown circle of raised earth, outlined in spring by a blaze of the gorse which surely may have given its name—*Castle d'Or*—to the Castle of Gold? Archaeological research has revealed that the site was inhabited as many as 2,000 years before the Romans came to Britain. It lay deserted for many years, and then—as befitted such a splendid site, commanding views of the accessible beaches of Par and the haven of Fowey—was settled again. A medieval palace arose, a wooden hall at its centre no less than 80 feet long and 36 feet wide : a palace fit for a king.

The king for whom it was raised may, it is thought, have been Gorlais, whose murder and the rape of whose wife Igraine by Uther Pendragon is at the very outset of the whole Arthurian legend. ('So King Uther lay with Igraine ... and begat on her that night Arthur.') But however that may be, it is difficult not to connect the Castle with King Mark; his stronghold, according to the early sources of the legend, lay in the parish of St. Sampson, Golant—at what is now Lantyne, but was in Domesday Book Lancien. Golant is a tiny hamlet on the west bank of the river Fowey, once served by the Lostwithiel-Fowey railway, one of the sadder of Dr. Beeching's victims in the West Country. At Golant there is still a church dedicated to St. Sampson, though consecrated as late as the early sixteenth century.

But long before its dedication there was a persistent story that the priest of the parish used to exhibit in his church a dress presented to it by Queen Iseult, and that she and King Mark used to worship there. After Iseult and Tristan had fallen in love, their flight took them through the forest of Moresk (Moreis in Domesday), which indeed lay, 12,000 acres of it, asprawl the country to the west of Castle Dore. Le Mal Pas, which Iseult crossed, survives as Malpas, near Truro; and westward again the quartz-scattered moors reflect surely the name of Le Blanche Lande, with Carlyon as the site of Tristan's birth-place, Caerleon.

Swinburne probably has the last word on the burial-place of the lovers:

> *Now where they sleep shall moon or sunlight shine*
> *Nor man look down for ever; none shall say,*
> *Here once, or here, Tristram and Iseult lay!*

But the romantic will find it difficult to resist the atmosphere of Castle Dore, and the witness of the dumb granite which perhaps (and how much of history is perhaps) once marked the lovers' grave.

More recently, the blunted circle of earth at Castle Dore saw an episode of English history which rivalled in coarseness and dull horror anything in the Arthurian legend—an episode difficult to reconcile with the peace of the rich dark hedges and full fields of this strip of land. It was in the summer of 1644 that the Earl of Essex (who had brought his Parliamentary army westward to relieve be-leaguered Plymouth) followed Sir Richard Grenville's retreating army down through Liskeard to Lostwithiel.

The Royalists were, as always, in a vast majority in Cornwall, and even the smallest of small boys was Cavalier rather than Roundhead. It was indeed a small boy who panted up to Grenville's camp to report that 'there were many a gay men in Lord Mohun's house at Boconnoc'. A Royalist scouting party went out, and took the house, with several important Parliamentary officers. Grenville advanced on Essex, cutting off his retreat; the latter hung on grimly at Lost-withiel, stabling his horses in the church (probably as much to protect them from sabotage and a nail in the hoof, as out of wanton blasphemy) and hoping for a rescue which never came. The Royalist Army was by now at Fowey; the means of rescue by sea was impossible.

Soon, a distinguished visitor looked over the Royalist defences. Richard Symonds, a King's officer, wrote in his diary for August 19:

'His Majestie, attended with his owne troope, Queene's troope, commanded by Captain Brett and sixty commanded troopers, went to Cliffe, a parish on this side of the river that runs to Listithiel, where Colonel Lloyd, the Quarter-Master Generall's regiment lyes to keepe the passe. The enemye keeps the passe on the other side at the parish of Glant [Golant]. From thence His Majestie went to Lanteglos to the manor house belonging to the Lord Mohun just over against Foye, where his royall person ventured to goe into a walke there which is within halfe musket shott from Foye, where a poore fisherman was killed in looking over, at the same time that His Majestie was in the walke and in the place where the King a little afore passed by....'

This venture of King Charles into the front line was less rash than it may seem: nowhere in the country was enthusiasm for his cause more wholehearted: so much so indeed that a year earlier the King had written a special letter to all the men in the county (it is still to be seen painted on boards, leaning dustily against the walls of some Cornish belfries) commending their 'great and eminent courage and patience' in his cause, and praising God for the 'many strange victories over their and our enemies, in despight of all human probability, and all imaginable disadvantages'.

God was still on the King's side. The Parliamentarians were getting desperately short of food, despite the fact that they had fallen on Menabilly and denuded it of everything edible—Jonathan Rashleigh lost 500 sheep and 100 lambs, 18 draught oxen, 20 milch cows and a bull, 30 fattened bullocks, 60 store bullocks, 40 horses, 80 hogs . . . and a year's supply of stored-up butter, cheese, beer, wine, pork, beef and bacon. But all this did not last long, and Essex's men were harassed by the implacable antagonism of the Cornish: one night a guard discovered a burning fuse within two inches of the powder of the Parliamentary ammunition train.

On August 30, Essex decided on a desperate move, and attempted a break-out. It was betrayed, and 50 Royalist musketeers lay in wait near Lostwithiel. But by some unspeakable confusion, 2,000 Parliamentarians trotted past that same cottage uninjured, and reached Plymouth and safety.

But that was Essex's only comfort. On the last day of August he and his exhausted, starving men stumbled up the steep hill from

Lostwithiel and along the Fowey road. Essex himself described the retreat:

'The wayes were so extreme foul with excessive rain and the harness for the drought horses so rotton that in the marching off, we lost three demi-culverins and a brass piece, and yet the Major-General [Skippon] fought in the rear all day, he being loth to lose those pieces, thirty horses were put to each of them, but could not move them, the night was so foul and the soldiers so tired that they were hardly to be kept to their colours....'

Within the circle of Castle Dore the Parliamentarians made their last stand. It was hopeless, and as night fell many men lost heart and straggled into the darkness. In the shambles, Essex slipped away to Fowey with Lord Robartes and one or two officers, and persuaded a fishing boat to take him to Plymouth. Next day, Skippon surrendered, and through heavy rain the tattered remnants of his army marched, or stumbled, back to Lostwithiel, 'prest all of a heap like sheep—so dirty and dejected as was rare to see, none of them except some few of their officers that did look any of us in the face'.

They ran the gauntlet of the Royalist army: any worthwhile clothing was seized from their backs, so that many were left naked to the rain. At Lostwithiel, the Cornish waited to steal what remained. As the prisoners left the town, few had boots on their feet. Of the 6,000 men to leave Castle Dore, only a thousand survived to the end of their march—Poole, in Dorset.

During the Civil War, Lostwithiel was still an important borough; now, amalgamated with St. Austell, though it still has its Mayor, its real importance has vanished, and it is difficult to remember how vital it once was to the life of the county, with its range of administrative buildings down by the busy quay: the 'Duchy Palace', with Stannary Gaol, Coinage Hall and Exchequer. Now there are a few ragged walls only, and the Exchequer Hall alone resisted the eighteenth-century demolition work; it is now a Masonic Hall.

The church has a beautiful, elegant and unique spire, and a peal of bells that has become very well-known through monthly broadcasts on the radio. But the main reason for stopping in the area is the ruin of Restormel Castle, a long mile eastward—'by far the most perfect example of military architecture in Cornwall', as Professor Pevsner puts it. Within living memory, the ruin was almost completely covered with ivy and creeper; etchings of the 1820s show tiny ladies and gentlemen quizzing the derelict pile with the civilised, distant admiration of those to whom, like Catherine Morland, a ruin was a folly whose main interest was as an attribute of landscape rather than as a remnant of history.

The ivy had time to gain a hold: even in 1530, when poor John Leland, Henry VIII's antiquary (his wits even then giving way) came to Restormel, it had been long decayed. Laboriously, he noted: 'Ther is a castel on an hil ... wher sumtymes the Erles of Cornewal lay. The base court is sore defacid. The fair large dungeon yet stondith. A chapel cast out of it, a newer work than it, and now onrofid.'

A mere 60 years later, Carew found the Castle even more dilapidated. The inhabitants of Lostwithiel were given to running out with a horse and cart, and picking out the more handsome pieces of stone to decorate their own houses. 'Certes', says Carew, 'it may move compassion that a palace so healthful for air, so delightful for prospect, so necessary for commodities, so fair (in regard of those days) for building, and so strong for defence, should in time of secure peace, and under the protection of his natural princes, be wronged with those spoilings than which it could endure no greater at the hands of any foreign and deadly enemy. For the park is disparked, the timber rooted up, the conduit pipes taken away, the roof made sale of, the planchings rotten, the walls fallen down, and the hewed stone of the windows, dourns and clavels plucked out to serve private buildings; only there remaineth an utter defacement to complain upon this unregarded distress....'

Dear Carew!—he had a concern for his country which would be a credit to any modern conservationist. And how delighted he would be to see Restormel today, as capably restored as the Ministry of Works can restore it. One needs only a touch of imagination to see the glory that once was here, where the Black Prince took over an elderly banked castle built by one Baldwin FitzTurstin, a new Norman landowner who bridged the Fowey just below Restormel, and threw up his defences on the hill. The Prince's surveyors, in 1337, found that in the 200 years since FitzTurstin had died, the castle had deteriorated: the kitchens were particularly ruinous, and the bakehouse and stables (for 20 horses) were falling down.

But there was a fine stone wall, put up by Robert de Cardinan at the end of the twelfth century, and the Black Prince had built a fine range of buildings inside it by the time he arrived to spend Christmas, 1362, at Restormel. Walking around the top of the wall, 27 feet up, one can look down on these rooms: private apartments for the lord and lady, a chapel (which once had as a centrepiece an image of the Virgin Mary sparkling with precious stones), a great hall with a wooden gallery overhanging the courtyard (handy for Shakespearean speeches of encouragement to the troops), storage rooms, and the kitchen with its vast fireplace, which attracted the attention of the Elizabethan surveyor, Norden, in 1584:

'If the proportion of necessarie offices in auntiente decayd buyldings may argue equall hospitalitie, here was noe waste ... and it is to be thought in those dayes they buylded for use and not as men now doe their great and glorious houses for ostentation, great halls and little meat, large chimneys and little smoak.' Things have never been what they were!

There are two features worth noticing in particular at Restormel: a staircase leading up in the thickness of the wall from inside a window recess of the lord's private room, to the sentry-walk. 'A secret stairway', the official guide calls it. I doubt it: a secret from whom, after all? An escape route?—but to the top of a high wall? No, just a convenience, I think; but a useful one for keeping an eye on one's servants. (*Quis custodiet . . . !*) And unusual, too, is the little shaft which leads from the sentry-walk down to a window in the great hall. No doubt a means by which the lord, at dinner, could instantly hear news of approaching horsemen from the sentry on duty 30 feet above him, in the clear cold night air, and lay out either an extra plate or his armour, according to the nature of the visitors.

The Cornish probably heaved a sigh of relief when the Black Prince caught the fever at Valladolid, resigned his principality (though not his dukedom, which was far too profitable) and eventually died. They had been too liable to sudden impressments to be very enthusiastic about the Prince, who tended to come to Cornwall only when he wanted more fodder for his French wars—able-bodied men, or horses, or money. In one year alone (1377) he had seized £2,219 7s. 9½d. of the county's total revenue of £3,415, for his own purposes. How much did his Cornish tenants contribute, I wonder, to that magnificent tomb in Canterbury Cathedral?

Restormel remained the seat of the visiting Dukes of Cornwall (and the elder son of every monarch since Edward III has been Duke of Cornwall automatically, since drawing his first breath). A Duke who remained happily absent (and was far from regal) was Piers Gaveston (the 'favourite', as the history books still nicely put it, of Edward II); but the Dukes have generally been more respectable, even if absentee landlordism has been the rule rather than the exception. And since the castle was not used as a Royal residence (and if it had been, would no doubt have been too expensive to maintain) it was allowed to crumble. At least now its restoration has made it one of the most accessible ruins in the county, and certainly one not to be missed.

The two 'great houses' of the area, both within easy reach of Lostwithiel (which as a matter of fact is a very good centre from which to make excursions into East Cornwall) are Boconnoc and Lanhydrock. Boconnoc, which housed Charles I during his Cornish visit in the Civil War, is not a very handsome house—but its grounds are very beautiful, laid out with all the commanding elegance of the eighteenth century. Thomas Pitt, Lord Camelford, supervised their design, and built one wing of the house; the other was built in 1709 by another Thomas Pitt, a Governor of Madras. Odd that Pitt, whose taste prompted the decoration of the gilt and mirrored gallery at Walpole's Strawberry Hill, should have been content with such a dull house at home. There is no evidence even of his 'finical, lady-like' manners, observed by Dr. Johnson's friend Mrs. Thrale. No, the house itself is worth a passing glance only; but the grounds are another matter, even the walls made interesting by the fragments of medieval windows and doorways which appear from time to time —all that remains of the medieval Boconnoc. The little private church behind the house has a chipped painted plaster royal coat-of-arms, beneath which no doubt Charles worshipped.

Lanhydrock is another matter—one of the grandest houses in Cornwall, built by Sir Richard Robartes, a tin and wool merchant from Truro, in the 1620s. Just after completing the house, he slipped £10,000 into the ready palm of Buckingham, and in return became a peer. Home he drove in triumph, over Respryn bridge (a century older than his handsome new house) and up a winding road through an avenue of sycamores. The view which met his eyes was different from ours, however: the neat little gate-house in granite was not finished until 1651, and the house itself is no longer set about a quadrangle. An old-fashioned house before it was completed, it was altered in 1780, and again in 1857 (by George Gilbert Scott, the most fashionable architect of his time); then, in 1881, came fire, gutting the whole of the house except the north wing.

Richard Coad, a Cornish architect from Liskeard, was in charge of rebuilding. He used local materials—granite from Lanlivery, walling stone from Bodmin, roofing slate from the great quarry at Delabole —and worked tactfully and well (though under a barrage of contradictory advice and orders from the then owner).

The new house was much more elaborate than the old: here was a butler's suite with sitting-room, bedroom, pantry and strong-room (with a bed for the pantry-boy placed across the door of the safe containing the silver!); rooms for housekeeper, maids, other servants; servants' hall, bakehouse, still-room, wine and beer cellars, gun-room, dairy, cold room, brushing-room, men- and maid-servants' bedrooms (separate staircases, of course). And a central heating system which is still in use.

The interior of the house has one great glory: the 116-foot-long gallery, with beautifully large windows throwing a good light on to the plaster barrel ceiling finished just before the Civil War, and showing in 24 panels incidents from Old Testament history, surrounded by a veritable zoo of birds and beasts placed in smaller panels. The carving is done with much more enthusiasm than finesse, but the simple joy of it all makes the room a warm and happy one. (A family of plasterers, the Abbots, of Frithelstock, near Bideford, was responsible.) Recently, the gallery has been used occasionally for chamber concerts and recitals; the acoustics are almost perfect, and the experience a delightful one.

Apart from the gallery, the visitor will find a fully equipped Victorian billiard-room (surprisingly few of these still survive with all their fittings), but really rather prosaic and slightly dull sitting-rooms and drawing-rooms. I am devoted to the very early penny-in-the-slot stamp machine in the inner hall; look after the pennies, as Mr. Paul Getty has shown, and the pounds will look after themselves.

In the little church tucked away behind the house, is an interesting bell—apparently a reproduction of a much older one, with a prayer carved on it for the soul of King Athelstan, who was in the Middle Ages thought to have founded Bodmin Priory. This is only one of several interesting bells in Cornwall: about 50 still surviving from pre-Restoration years, and here and there fifteenth-century bells (usually a trio) still peal out—as at Caerhayes, Landewednack and Gunwallow, for instance. The Commissioners who visited Gunwallow in 1551 noted the *iij bellys* which are there today, complete with their inscriptions: *Plebs omnis plaudit ut me tam sepius audit—All people cheer when they me hear.*

There are a good number of enthusiastic teams of bell-ringers in Cornwall, who on annual outings still tour from church to church ringing peals; and since there is usually a pub next the church, the peals become more and more enthusiastic as the day wears on. Ringers were usually given free beer on festival days, in times past, and a number of shattered bells used to lie on the earthern floors of church towers as witness, sledgehammers having been taken to them in moments of stress or delight.

The gardens outside Lanhydrock House are worth spending an afternoon in. The formerly elaborate flower garden to the south-east is now planted mainly with roses; 38 clipped yew trees alternate with some splendid bronze urns which once stood in the Bois de Bologne. Elsewhere, the higher garden has many flowering shrubs (including a magnificent magnolia), and a little thatched pavilion covered with flowering quince, firethorn and a trumpet vine. Rhododendrons, of course; cotoneasters; a tunnel of magnolias; limes, beeches and pines; and further off, the Great Wood. Really, one of the show gardens of the county, and ideal for a timeless stroll on a summer afternoon.

CHAPTER FOUR

East Cornwall

The triangle of land between Lostwithiel, Newquay and Padstow, is quiet and unassuming, except where (especially around St. Breock Downs) it becomes rather wild and open, a taste of Bodmin Moor; and where, around the coast-line, even on the calmest day there is a hint of menace in the white line where the sea meets submerged or half-submerged rocks. The long breakers welcomed by surfers farther west are not nearly so friendly here, for they have wicked under-tows; as I write, I hear that on one afternoon 20 bathers have been rescued from the sea near Padstow. They were lucky. I have had one or two memories myself not far removed from the experience John Betjeman records in his poem about the beach at Green-away, on the north coast of Cornwall (to which he is devoted, and which he has described with great vividness):

> There were the stile, the turf, the shore,
> The safety line of shingle beach,
> With every stroke I struck the more
> The backwash sucked me out of reach.
>
> Back into what a water-world
> Of waving weed and waiting claws?
> Of writhing tentacles uncurled
> To drag me to what dreadful jaws?

I have been neglecting the north coast—because, I suppose, there are more interesting places to visit on the south coast. But one must admit that for sheer beauty of land- and sea-scape, the north coast all the way from St. Ives to Bude (and for that matter on to Bridge-water Bay) remains unbeaten. There are good roads running either on or near the coast all the way from St. Ives: the B3301 to Redruth, B3285 from St. Agnes to Goonhavern, then the A3075 to Newquay;

the ravishingly beautiful B3276 on to Padstow, and then across the estuary (which you cross upstream at Wadebridge) the B3314 and B3263 through Tintagel, eventually joining the A39. There are no coastal roads like these on the south coast, and at almost every point where they dip inland, one can find little by-roads leading off on the left to such places as St. Agnes Head or Holywell Bay, Treyarnon Bay or Trevose Head, Portquin, Port Isaac, Crackington Haven or Morwenstow. Almost all of them are worth following.

The sheer contrast of sandy inlet, rocky headland, soft warm curve of green hill against the sea, or vertiginous cliff, makes the north coast exhilarating and perhaps unparalleled in the whole of England. (This strange harmony of contrasts is indeed one of the great delights of Cornwall as a whole.)

One of the benefits of the north coast is that (apart from Newquay, which is a special case, and perhaps Padstow and Tintagel) it does not attract quite so many tourists as the rest of the county. Bays like Porthcothan and Trevone can still be fairly quiet. But round Trevose Head past Constantine Bay (not the Roman Constantine, by the way, but the Cornish St. Cystennyn, said to have succeeded Arthur as King of the British) Padstow is a different matter at least on one day of the year, for here every year the Padstow Hobby Horse cavorts through the town in the most high-spirited of all Cornish May Day festivals. The Helston Furry Dance has become 'nice'; the Hobby Horse retains some of its ancient gusto and lustiness.

At two in the morning the song can begin:

> With a merry ring adieu the joyful spring,
>   For summer is a-come unto day;
> How happy are those little birds which merrily do sing
>   In the merry morning of May ...

Then through the streets and on to the quay comes the Horse himself, with a strange, painted mask and a vast hooped skirt of black tarpaulin under which a girl may be trapped if she is not quick. With his attendant waving a club, he dances through the town, until at midday he bows his head in a strangely touching submission, the attendant lays his club across it, and

O where is St. George? O where is he, O?
He's down in his long boat all on the salt sea, O....

Then the horse revives, and the dance begins again. The Padstow Horse seems the last of a number of horses which once jogged the length of England—the Hooden Horse of Kent, the Mari Llwyd of Wales; there were others in Romania, Poland, the Basque country. Now, Padstow's remains, with an elemental force of some kind driving him on, and with a purity and grace and magic which the increasing crowds, the multiplying litter of ice-cream papers and cigarette-packets, cannot dampen. It is the most rewarding of all Cornwall's annual ceremonies.

On an 'ordinary' day, Padstow is just another Cornish fishing-port, a group of houses on its quay, with little streets straggling untidily up the valley to St. Petroc's Church and Prideaux Place. Sir Nicholas Prideaux (who died in 1627) has a pretty monument in the church, with a little plump grinning child standing on an old man's shoulder, and four life-sized carvings of Sir Nicholas' children facing their parents across a set of prayer desks.

Carew knew and liked Sir Nicholas and his house—in his day 'a new and stately house [which] taketh a full and large prospect of the town, haven and country adjoining, to all which his wisdom is a stay, his authority a direction'. The house is a handsome one, but not open to the public.

Not only the church at Padstow is dedicated to St. Petroc: so is the parish church at Bodmin, and both towns were at one time called Petrockstow, to the great confusion of historians. Padstow has also been referred to in the past as Lodenek and Aldestow! Its harbour lies a couple of miles from the mouth of the estuary, and apart from some difficulty with sand-banks (by which it was plagued by a mermaid rejected by a Padstow sailor), is the safest harbour on the coast. In the eighteenth century, on one map was inscribed the words: 'Padstow: by its Situation at the Mouth of the River Camel in the Bristol Channel, lies very convenient for Commerce with Ireland. The Inhabitants of this Town, for the Love of Mirth and Good Cheer, give rise to the proverbial phrase of the Good Fellowship of Padstow.'

Padstow in the sixteenth century, indeed, had been one of the ports from which men and supplies had set off to the Irish wars; two

88

boats sailed from its harbour to the siege of Calais. It cannot be this trafficking with overseas, surely, that gave it a strangely un-Cornish aspect? I think it may simply be the sand: sand as bright yellow as in any child's colouring-book, in great shoals across the estuary to Rock, and on that side of the river also; quite untypical of the coast and county.

On the way to Wadebridge one passes near St. Breock, where Tregeagle lies buried: 'John Tregeagle of Trevorder, Esqr., 1679.' What this poor Tregeagle had done to deserve his reputation one cannot conjecture; but his name has attached itself to one of the most persistent legends of Cornwall—a legend some elements of which are at least a thousand years older than the historical man.

He must, one supposes, have been an unpleasant fellow, or the legend would not have attached itself to him. A persistently unjust steward, perhaps, for the Robartes family at Lanhydrock, he is said to have murdered his wife, his children, and his sister, but gave a proportion of the small fortune he stole from his master to the Church, so that at his death priests managed to repel the devils who called for his soul, and interred him at St. Breock. But a few years later, a Lanhydrock tenant needed Tregeagle's evidence in a law suit, and took the uncustomary course of raising his spirit, which testified from the witness box.

The devils were still in wait, and the best the priests could do to preserve the soul of their generous benefactor was to give it perpetual penance. So they led Tregeagle's spirit to Dozmare Pool, on Bodmin Moor—a large natural lake on top of the moor near Jamaica Inn—gave him a limpet shell with a hole in it, and told him to empty the Pool. He persevered for more years than one might expect, but during a furious thunderstorm fled from the place, chased by the devils, and took refuge at Roche Rock, where he pushed his head in at an upper window. After an uncomfortable few centuries during which his exposed rump was visited by whatever torments the devils might devise, two clergymen came to his rescue with another penance. He was to spin useful ropes—from the sand of the Padstow beaches.

His continual wails of torment disturbed the sleep of the people of Padstow, and once more he removed—first to Helston, and then to Land's End, where he is engaged at the present time in trying to sweep the sands from Porthcurno Cove—in direct competition with the Atlantic rollers, which fill the cove up again as fast as it is emptied. What might sound to a sceptical ear like the roaring of a nor'-easterly wind is really anguished Tregeagle voicing his discontent.

On, then, past his empty (presumably) tomb, to Wadebridge, and across the finest medieval bridge in England : 320 feet long, with over 17 arches, put up in 1468. The bridge replaced the ford from which the town took its name, and across which travellers would cross on the road to Bodmin, the county town of Cornwall.

The town gained reflected glory, no doubt, from its association with St. Petroc, who was of outstanding importance among the Celtic saints. His life is much embroidered by the medieval writers who first set down his history; but he seems to have come from South Wales to Padstow, and made the Camel estuary the centre of his monastic and missionary activities. Later in his life, he is said to have withdrawn to the remoteness of a hermitage on the wild Bodmin Moor, and by the eleventh century Bodmin had become the centre of his cult, and an important shrine containing his relics was at the heart of his church there until 1171, when a Breton priest stole them away and took them across to St. Méen.

The fury of the Bodmin citizens had the kind of intensity shown by the Scots when speaking of the Stone of Scone, and they made such a fuss that Henry II sent a band of soldiers to recover the relics, which were returned to Bodmin amid scenes of great rejoicing (echoed for centuries each July 7, when a large piece of wood decorated with flowers would be carried to church for a celebratory service; after which the congregation leaped as one man on to their horses and rode to the moors above the town for a spirited afternoon of racing). The relics have long since disappeared, presumably for good.

The church itself was no doubt overshadowed by the shrine at least until it was rebuilt in 1469-72, as the largest church in the county. Nearly every parishioner subscribed to the rebuilding fund (the Vicar gave a year's salary), and about 20 masons were employed at 6d. a day. The result is splendid indeed : over 150 feet long and 65 feet wide, with a tower that is still impressive, and must have been more so before its spire was destroyed in 1699.

Bodmin itself commands little affection, partly perhaps because it was the judicial centre of Cornwall, with an assize court put up in the mid-nineteenth century, unobtrusive and unimpressive. It was Bodmin Moor, which comes right to the eastern boundary of the town, which was responsible for the failure of the king's judges to come any farther west than Launceston until 1715; the law officers had to travel east across the moor, frozen and aggressively un-pleasant in mid-winter. By a happy coincidence, the very year after the House of Commons decided that Assizes must in future be held at Bodmin, 'the roads and wayes from Launceston to Bodmyn be levelled, and the trees and hedges cut fit for travelling with coaches &c'.

That was in 1715; but the county gaol remained at Launceston until 1780, when 'a larger and more commodious County Prison' was built at Bodmin. It is now partly ruined, and partly converted into a nightclub, with jukeboxes and strippers bellowing and bumping and grinding in the very cells where between 1785 and 1882, there were 50 hangings. In 1787 a man was hanged for stealing a watch; five were hanged for sheep-stealing, five for burglary, two for shop-breaking, two for housebreaking, two for forgery, and one for the slaughter of a ram and the theft of part of the carcass.

The Cornish were no more given to lenity than any other men in the bloodthirsty eighteenth century; yet even they drew the line at hanging smugglers, and at least one Polperro man condemned in Bodmin court was taken away quietly at night, in a rattling cart over the misty moor, to be hanged safely at Newgate before he could be rescued by an indignant posse of his fellow-smugglers.

These days the A30 glides smoothly over the moor from Launces-ton to Bodmin, and no one need fear the journey—except in a sud-den fog. One should choose one's time to climb Rough Tor or Brown Willy (the latter, at 1,375 feet, the highest hill in the county). And it might be remembered, too, that there are stories of whole horses vanishing under their riders' legs into quagmires, with a low sucking of peaty water; followed, later, by their owners. Look before you step.

The main attraction of Bodmin Moor is, I think, in wandering about on it; but all the same there are one or two *places* worth visit-ing—for instance, Blisland, not far from Bodmin, with its little

Church of St. Protus and St. Hyacinth. A church which sent John Betjeman into a mild hysteria of delight in his *First and Last Loves*. He quotes Sir Ninian Cooper, and calls it 'a church to bring you to your knees when you first enter it'. Agreeing, one still wonders why, for it is not a church of any conventional beauty: its arcade leaning drunkenly southwards; an 1896 rood screen; a mock-Renaissance altar; a Grinling Gibbons-style pulpit … and yet it all comes together as an inevitable and charming whole.

Two miles north, over the De Lank river, are two clapper bridges, at Bradford, with their huge slabs of stone looking as if they will be in place until Doomsday. The De Lank river rises between Rough Tor and Brown Willy, right on top of the moor; and near Brown Willy rises, too, the River Fowey, which trickles along beside a winding road from Bolventor to St. Cleer; a pretty valley, and halfway down it a set of low waterfalls, where the clear stream bounces over a series of rounded boulders. Ideal for a picnic, and when the hunt meets there, red coats against the green valley, it all looks like an old-fashioned Christmas card (the smell of blood, though, somewhere about).

Between Bodmin and Bolventor the moors are speckled with boulders, some of them obviously carefully positioned by human hands, but when and for what purpose one can only guess. One small group formed a series of rough huts in which, two centuries ago, lived the strange and sympathetic figure of Daniel Gumb—a natural hippy if ever there was one—the son of a labourer who dimly heard of Newton's discoveries about the planets, and decided to spend his life, too, studying the skies. He lacked the genius of Sir Isaac, but not the application, and after he had built his house on the moor, lived there with his wife Florence, astronomer and astrologer, until his death.

Even now one can just see, on the flat surfaces of the stones which covered his head, strange markings—some geometric, some algebraic, some astrological—which this strange old man carved there. A good few legends must have swarmed around his head during his lifetime and after; just as they collected around Dozmare Pool, not far away, near Jamaica Inn, the coaching inn which Daphne du Maurier made the centrepiece of her romance.

'The country people', said Carew, 'held many strange conceits of

this pool, as, that it did ebb and flow, that it had a whirlpool in the midst thereof, and that a faggot once thrown thereinto was taken up at Fowey haven, six miles distant.' I was told some of these legends, as a small boy; just as I learned that Dozmary was the scene of the last act of the Arthurian legend, where Sir Bedivere threw Excalibur shining through the air, and where

> rose an arm,
> *Clad in white samite, mystic, wonderful,*
> *And caught him by the hilt, and brandished him*
> *Three times, and drew him under in the mere.*

Well, Tennyson may have had the Pool in mind; but otherwise the connection seems tenuous. Dozmary—too shallow for swimming, too small for sailing, too deep for paddling—is more an excellent example of natural landscape gardening than anything else.

Here, at the centre of Bodmin Moor, one begins to feel the pull of 'old country'—of moorland only scratched by man. It is a feeling which grows more intense when, travelling east, one reaches after ten or 12 miles the larger, rough tract of Dartmoor. Although Hardy was writing specifically neither of Dartmoor nor (certainly) Bodmin Moor, the opening pages of *The Return of the Native* capture perfectly the atmosphere of both, at their grimmest and most impressive:

'The place became full of a watchful intentness now; for when other things sank brooding to sleep the heath appeared slowly to wake and listen. Every night its titanic form seemed to await something; but it had waited thus, unmoved, during so many centuries, through the crises of so many things, that it could only be imagined to await one last crisis—the final overthrow.... Twilight combined with the scenery of Egton Heath to evolve a thing majestic without severity, impressive without showiness, emphatic in its admonitions, grand in its simplicity.... Only in summer days of highest feather did its mood touch the level of gaiety. Intensity was more usually reached by way of the solemn than by way of the brilliant, and such a sort of intensity was often arrived at during winter darkness, tempests, and mists. Then Egton was aroused to reciprocity; for the storm was its lover, and the wind its friend.'

13 *Brunel's Saltash Bridge (1859), Plymouth*

Between Bodmin Moor and the north coast, the important place is Tintagel, firmly connected by legend with King Arthur and the Arthurian saga. Archaeologists have never been eager to support the theory, and indeed until fairly recently held that the claim originated not earlier than the first half of the twelfth century, when Geoffrey of Monmouth mentioned Tintagel Castle as Arthur's residence. However traces have now been found of a celtic monastery near the medieval chapel of St. Juliot.

This celtic missionary, who arrived in about 500 A.D., built his cell at Tintagel, disregarding the marked inhospitality of the uncouth cliffs (as Carew called them). After a few years, a flourishing monastery grew up in buildings scattered over the surrounding countryside. A hall with a good heating system, a steam bath, a rock pool for cold plunges, a well, a garden, a chapel, a cemetery—remnants of all of them survive.

But by the time of Domesday Book, the monastery had vanished, and it was Earl Richard, the younger brother of Henry III, who began serious building here in the first half of the thirteenth century. Originally, what is now the island was really a promontory: Geoffrey of Monmouth in his *History of the Kings of Britain*, finished in 1136, described the then rudimentary castle as an impregnable fortress:

'The castle is built high above the sea, which surrounds it on all sides, and there is no other way in except that offered by a narrow isthmus of rock. Three armed soldiers could hold it against you even if you stood there with the whole kingdom of Britain at your side.'

Gradually, through the fourteenth and fifteenth centuries, the sea ate away at the isthmus, and eventually only a bridge connected the two parts of the castle—upper and lower ward on the mainland, and inner ward on the island itself, surrounding the twelfth-century Great Hall. By the sixteenth century, the island was deserted; the bridge broke and vanished, and a few shepherds went rabbiting or a few fishermen spread their nets to dry there. That was all.

The ruins are not—like those at Restormel or even Launceston—clean-cut enough to give a very good idea of what the fortress can have been like. Building has been placed on top of building, walls have been knocked down, rebuilt, altered; for instance, the Great Hall, which in 1337 was ruinous and unroofed, was replaced seven or eight years later by a smaller hall; and by the time the castle was being used as a prison (at the end of the same century) another range of buildings stood on that same site.

The Ministry of Public Building and Works has produced an excellent guide, however, by C. Ralegh Radford, which makes all as clear as can be. So a sense of history can be satisfied at Tintagel, almost as readily as a sense of romance. Tennyson jotted in his notebook, on his visit, 'Black cliffs and caves and storms and wind.' And he returned twice, the last time at the height of his fame, after the publication of *Idylls of the King* had made Tintagel a focus for tourists. Perhaps indeed it was out of a sense of gratitude for a new source of income that an old woman is recorded to have rushed out of her cottage there and recited passages from his Arthurian poems at the Laureate as he walked down towards the beach.

The village itself is ugly almost beyond belief; King Arthur's Hotel is almost worth a special detour, it is so spectacularly, massively unbeautiful. But there is also the Old Post Office, a jolly little manor house with a central hall, open to the roof timbers, and probably built in the early fifteenth century. It was used as a post office as early as 1844, and the National Trust has recently refurnished the old post room as a Victorian village post office, complete with just such a Spagnoletti's Telegraph Receiver as the sub-postmaster, Mr. William Cobbledick Balkwill, would have operated in 1890.

Swinburne, as well as Tennyson, loved Tintagel (especially for its rolling breakers and the lowering heights of its cliffs); and three or four miles along the coast, Thomas Hardy set his novel *A Pair of Blue Eyes*. Hardy had come to St. Juliot, just over two miles up the river Volancy from Boscastle, as a consultant architect to look after the restoration of St. Julietta Church there. During 1871 and 1872, he conducted the restoration (some of his drawings are still to be seen in the church), and courted the rector's sister, whom he married two years later. She was a terrible woman (who worked hard to have the marvellous *Jude the Obscure* suppressed, on the grounds of obscenity), and it was not a happy match. There is a tablet in Mrs. Hardy's memory in the church. Better to forget her. But *A Pair of Blue Eyes* is a moving, melancholy record of Hardy's love affair, and of his love of this district, too: it has some wonderful topographical passages.

Nothing could be more different from the roughness of this tract of coast than the countryside between Bodmin Moor and the southern coastline. The rich green of the Looe valley, for instance, or even the cliffs between Fowey and Polperro—as different from the cliffs of Tintagel as can be imagined, for these are kinder cliffs, the plants and grasses that mask them less buffeted by winds and weather.

Polperro can scarcely be commended any longer as the 'ideal holiday village' it was in the 1920s and '30s. Then it was still in part a fishing village, and I remember much more recently than that, seeing the quay a moving silver raft of stranded fishes. But now, the tourist industry has taken over completely: dust clouds roll over the carpark at the head of the valley (no car is allowed into the village itself without a pass), and the tiny streets are crowded with visitors buying trashy trinkets. Really, if one is ever seriously tempted to take against the whole human race, it is in the summer at Polperro.

And yet it is simply not true to say that the village has been ruined; despite the crude hoardings, the masses of overhead cables, if one goes there in the off-season, something of the magic remains. How beautiful the village could still be if some planning authority had been established, say, in 1920, and imposed proper controls on advertising, electrification, television aerials. . . .

I would like to be able to commend Dr. Jonathan Couch's *History of Polperro*, the best local history I know; but alas, it has been out of print for a hundred years, and by the nature of things is unlikely to be republished. All the same, it is a classic of its kind, written by a kindly old man who, besides being the village doctor, was an eminent natural historian, who would rush to the quayside to paint meticulous watercolour sketches of fish whose colours were still undimmed by death, and had been brought ashore in pails of seawater specifically so that he should see them in their natural glory. He wrote and illustrated what was for years the standard work on British fishes, and in some respects still is so.

'The Old Doctor' (who remembered watching Tennyson walking through Polperro carrying the first umbrella he had ever seen) lovingly recorded local legends, as well as the sometimes querulous, sometimes extrovert and lively behaviour of his patients. He died, universally beloved, at his home by the little bridge over the stream that runs down the valley through the village; and his grandson, 'Q',

made Couch's House the home of the hero of his novel *Nicky-Nan,
Reservist*. The 'Polpier' of that book is a beautiful recreation of Polperro as 'Q' himself remembered it just after the turn of the century.
Occasionally, *Nicky-Nan* turns up on the 'remaindered' shelves of
bookshops, and anyone who wonders what life in Cornwall was like
before the tourist invasion, before the transistor on the beach and
the influence of the Sunday colour supplements on the paintwork,
should read it.

The two Looes—West and East—form a sort of miniature Newquay. The cream teas are no worse than anywhere else; the speed-
boat trips round the bay no less vertiginous. The bay certainly is a
lovely one, but the Looes themselves are unremarkable; the only
thing historians ever remark upon has vanished—the bridge which
spanned the river until 1853; built in 1411, it had 13 arches, and
must indeed have been a marvellous sight. More recently, on fair
and feast days, Looe was worth a visit for the goings-on on the quayside: only a century ago a visitor found a booth-theatre where he
could see *The Midnight Assassin, or, The Dumb Witness* and, next
night, *The Vampire's Feast, or, The Rifled Tomb*—both performed
in broad Cornish!

Not far from Talland, between Polperro and Looe, still stands
Trelawne, a sixteenth-century house (though at least a part of it is
thirteenth century). Here lived the Trelawny family (including
Shelley's and Byron's eccentric friend, Edward), and here originated
the Cornish 'national anthem':

> *And have they fixed the where and when?*
> *And shall Trelawny die?*
> *Here's twenty thousand Cornishmen*
> *Will know the reason why.*

The song was included in one of his collections of Cornish ballads
by R. S. Hawker, but though he may have originated the version we
know, the song itself was much older—and probably originated
long before the imprisonment of the Seven Bishops (one of them Sir
Jonathan Trelawny) which is always said to have prompted it. A
much earlier Trelawny, John, was imprisoned in the Tower in 1627,
and it is probably his health that the original ballad-monger was

worried about. He need not have been; John Trelawny was released and given a baronetcy!

Stephen Hawker, who collected *Trelawny*, was for some years Vicar of Morwenstow, back on the north coast. The village is still attractive, because still remote; crimson and gold with heather and gorse during the summer, a valley over which the Eagle's Crag towers to 450 feet above the sea, protecting St. John's Church, with—surprisingly—a Norman arcade and south door (not many of those in Cornwall; St. German's, the cathedral of Cornwall in Anglo-Saxon times, has more Norman architecture about it than any other in the county). Nearby is the Vicarage, which Mr. Hawker built, its chimneys imitating the towers of the various churches he had been connected with, and the kitchen chimney a copy of his mother's tomb!

Hawker was a poet, believed in witchcraft and the evil eye, and was given to practical jokes (he once sat on the cold rocks of Bude, stark naked except for an oilskin tail, imitating a mermaid to great effect). He dressed habitually in a claret-coloured coat with long tails, a blue fisherman's jersey with a red cross knitted on it at the point where the soldier's spear pierced Jesus' side, and black socks knitted specially for him from the wool of a favourite sheep.

Hawker was in his study one night when a visitor was announced, and 'a tall, swarthy man with an eye like a sword' entered the room. It was Tennyson. The two men got on splendidly, even before Hawker realised who his visitor was. When the poet remarked on the remoteness of the village, the Vicar quoted *Locksley Hall*:

> *Locksley Hall, that in the distance overlooks the*
> *sandy tracts,*
> *And the hollow ocean-ridges roaring into cataracts.*
> *Many a night from yonder ivied casement, ere I*
> *went to rest,*
> *Did I look on great Orion sloping slowly to the*
> *West.*
> *Many a night I saw the Pleiads, rising thro' the*
> *mellow shade,*
> *Glitter like a swarm of fireflies, tangled in a*
> *silver braid.*

'Why, that man seems to be your favourite poet,' said Tennyson. 'Not mine only, but all England's,' was the reply. Whereupon Tennyson revealed himself, and the two men spent most of the night discussing the Arthurian legend, and Hawker told Tennyson stories of the fearful storms which could batter the coast, after which he would have to bury the tortured bodies of wrecked seamen; and not only that, but send a man with a basket to gather pieces of flesh cut from the bodies by the razored rocks. Tennyson must have remembered the talk when he wrote of the waves, after the battle in *The Passing of Arthur*, rolling

> in among dead faces, to and fro
> Swaying the helpless hands, and up and down
> Tumbling the hollow helmets of the fallen.

We are now in the borderland of Devon and Cornwall, with one more town of consequence to visit: Launceston, for many years the judicial centre of the county, and during Tudor times a town drenched with blood. In the Middle Ages this was Cornwall's most important town, with its castle—apart perhaps from Restormel— the most important castle. It lies on the side of a steep hill, the market square pinched between the remains of the castle and one of the most beautiful churches in the West Country.

Launceston Castle (the town, by the way, is pronounced 'Lanson') was built by one of the brothers of William the Conqueror, Robert of Mortain, rewarded for his help with the Conquest by the Earldom of Cornwall. It was his choice of Launceston as a headquarters which gave the town an importance which lasted well into the middle of the last century.

On top of the commanding hill above the little town, Earl Robert threw up a castle mound, and surrounded it by the usual palisade. A tower within this made an excellent fort for last-stand battles; and below it was a little square enclosure for everyday living. But it was a prefabricated castle built on the cheap—Earl Robert set aside less than £20 a year for its upkeep—and it was the ubiquitous and immensely wealthy Earl Richard who thoroughly improved the site, in the early thirteenth century.

When the Black Prince was made Duke, his surveyors visited Launceston as well as Restormel, and found the former in an even worse state than the latter. 'A certain hall with two cellars [which] need re-roofing, a sufficient kitchen attached to the said hall, a small upstairs hall called the earl's chamber with a chamber and a little chapel, whose walls are of timber and plaster, and the timber thereof is almost disjointed. And two chambers above the two gates sufficiently covered with lead, one old and decayed little hall for a constable with a chamber and cellar and a small kitchen attached. There is also a chapel in good order apart from the windows which are decayed, two stables for ten horses, a gaol badly and inadequately covered with lead, and another prison called "the Larder" weak and almost useless.'

The Black Prince put certain repairs in train, and ordered the townspeople to keep their pigs from rooting about and undermining the castle walls. The prison remained in a state of disrepair, and if anything got worse; it is the prison, indeed, I am forced to remember when I visit Launceston, for it became notorious. George Fox, the founder of the Quakers, was thrown into a small room by the gateway in 1656, for refusing to remove his hat when arraigned for distributing tracts; he called it *Doomsdale*. And at a seat outside it, the Sheriff of the county received his prisoners. Poor fellows: the prison reformer John Howard, as late as 1779, found that 'the prison is a room or passage, 23½ feet by 7½, with only one window 2 feet by 1½; and three dungeons or cages on the side opposite the window; these are about 6½ feet deep, one 9 feet long; one about 8; one not 5; this last for women. They are all very offensive. No chimney; no water; no sewers; damp earth floors.... I once found the prisoners chained two or three together. Their provisions were put down to them through a hole (9 inches by 8) in the floor of the room above (used as a chapel).'

It was probably even more noisome in 1576, when Cuthbert Mayne and over a score of others were brought after the surprise raid on Golden. Here, he was condemned. The night before his execution, loaded with chains and in the filth of his cell, he disputed with his judges and with ministers. Next day he was dragged on a hurdle to the gibbet in the market-place, and cruelly killed.

The scene always comes to my mind whenever I visit Launceston;

which is quite unfair, for it is a charming town, full of ups and downs, and ins and outs. One of the most delightful (albeit creepy) houses in the town is Dockover, an Elizabethan house off Angel Hill, which unbelievably was the main road into Launceston—third class passengers walking, no doubt. In the dining-room hang portraits of Nicholas and Elizabeth Herle, who lived in the house during the eighteenth century, when Herle was twice Mayor. In 1714, Elizabeth died (as her memorial stone recorded) 'by starvation or other unlawful mean'. And now, Nicholas (sometimes seen in the main hall of Dockover) plays a flute quietly upstairs when someone is about to die—always the same tune, a madrigal.

Every owner of Dockacre House gives his successor a walking stick; these are kept in the attic, in a sack, and if they are not put away in a certain order, they rattle noisily about putting themselves to rights.

Charles Causley, who lives in Launceston, has a splendid poem about the haunting; and indeed it is inadvisable to visit Launceston without his poems about one, for I have never known a town whose peculiar atmosphere has been better recorded by a living poet. Indeed, he has single-handedly revived the old custom by which children throw pebbles on to the back of a reclining granite carving of St. Mary Magdalene, on the wall of her Church in Launceston, for good luck.

The church was built by Sir Henry Trecarrel, after the death of his only son (at the age of four) had discouraged him from finishing his mansion at Trecarrel, about five miles south of the town. Causley describes the church, and the carvings which decorate it:

> *While Flodden was fought and the Frenchmen fell low*
> *And Cortes was conquering Mexico,*
> *When Wolsey was Generalissimo*
> *They hammered away at the holy chateau.*
>
> *When the sun in the summer is spreading his hood*
> *The beggar still sulks in the starving mud,*
> *The pelican glides with a gift of blood*
> *And the eagle ascends to the throne of good.*

Where winter descends with her smudging snow
The nardus and pomegranate grow,
And through the forest the frozen doe,
The greyhound, the griffin and honey-bear go.

The immortal yew and the frigid oak
Stand about Martin slicing his cloak,
And George (on a pony) tries to invoke
The dragon, making crystal smoke.

Now the Magdalen lies on a mica strand
Spreading her hair with an idle hand,
And ready to play at her command
Is a sawing sixteenth century band....

Trecarrel itself is now a farm, with a chapel standing lonely in a field, bare of everything except wishes. The great hall was used until fairly recently as a store-cum-barn; now, it has been cleared, and is in a beautiful state of preservation, wonderfully light and airy and with the most noble proportions. Certainly worth a drive through the lush countryside, to see; and notice too the large chunks of carefully carved granite which would have decorated the finished manor, but now lie in the long grass, or form part of a little garden, or act as hopping-posts for geese and ducks.

Trecarrel might have been a very great house indeed, in a small but determined way. Right in this borderland between Cornwall and Devon, stands one of the real great houses of the county, and perhaps the one most worth visiting: 14 miles north of Plymouth, it is Cotehele, built mostly in the sixteenth century, but which grew with the ages—a tower here, a window there—so that it seems an organic part of the landscape.

Hilaria de Cotehele owned the original manor, and brought it into the Edgcumbe family when, in 1353, she married a William Edgcumbe, whose family came from Milton Abbot, near Tavistock. The house was a small one, though by 1411 it had its own chapel (not the present one, which dates from later in the fifteenth century).

Sir Richard Edgcumbe, who owned the house during the second half of that century, was its most heroic, filibustering inhabitant; he joined the Duke of Buckingham's revolt against Richard III, and conducted a violent feud with a neighbour, Robert Willoughby of Bere Ferrers—though they made it up after a little mutual servant-beating and ambushing, and became firm friends.

Edgcumbe, after Buckingham's execution, lay low at Cotehele—but was tracked down by one of the most feared men in the West Country, Sir Henry Trenowth of Bodrugan, a butcher for Richard III, who certainly seems to have had in truth all the treachery, violence and sadism attributed to his master. Cotehele was surrounded: but Edgcumbe quietly slit a sentry's throat, and tore off through the grounds, Trenowth at his heels. Reaching a spot 70 feet above the River Tamar, Edgcumbe wrapped his cap around a stone, and threw it into the water. Trenowth and his men, Carew reports, 'looking down after the noise, and seeing his cap swimming thereon, supposed that he had desperately drowned himself, and gave over their further hunting'. Edgcumbe slipped over to Brittany; but returned some years later, and built on the spot a chapel to SS. George and Thomas à Becket, which still stands.

After Bosworth Field, Edgcumbe was made a knight and Controller of Henry VII's household; he was also given the estates of his enemy, Trenowth, who he in turn chased: more fatally, for the latter took a real leap into the sea—at Bodrugan's Leap, between Mevagissy and the Dodman Head. He has not been heard of since.

Sir Richard spent little time at Cotehele, for he became one of the king's most travelled councillors. But he did begin enlarging the house, and his son Piers carried on with the work, completing for instance the Great Hall: slightly old-fashioned for its time, using the medieval form of roofing rather than the modern hammerbeams such as Cardinal Wolsey had recently installed at Hampton Court.

A few more additions were made to the building in the next hundred years or so; but after 1750, the family deserted the house for their other estate at Mount Edgcumbe, and Cotehele has only been spasmodically inhabited ever since. But it has always been meticulously maintained, and remains a beautifully preserved Tudor house, with a collection of late Stuart and early Georgian furniture that has never left it. It is a rather creepy place—heavy tapestries, four-posters, a vicious slit in the wall of the Great Hall (from which it is possible to see, and no doubt execute, with a swift bow-shot, unwelcome visitors), and a ghostly steel mirror dating from 1625 (spectacularly early for such a convenience) in which I always expect to see a grey Tudor face peering over my shoulder.

Outside, a set of comfortable grounds, with a ruined tower (a folly?—useful for sending signals, it has been suggested, from Cotehele to Mount Edgcumbe), and some lovely old sycamores and yews. At the right season, there are almost more daffodils here than I have seen anywhere at one place together!

Mount Edgcumbe, in which the Edgcumbes preferred to live after the middle of the eighteenth century, stands nine miles or so away from Cotehele, on the Rame Head peninsula, facing across the South to Plymouth. Sir Richard Edgcumbe built it in 1547-54, with four corner towers and a high hall 'rising in the midst above the rest', as Carew said, who visited it as a child. Sir Richard drew up the plans himself, and told his builders strictly that they were to follow 'always ... the devyse, advyse and plan'. It was a very modern house, compared to Cotehele, and as much for its position as its design, exceptionally beautiful. The story goes, indeed, that the Spanish Admiral Medina Sidonia glimpsed the house from his flagship as he sailed up the channel at the head of the Armada, and marked it out as his future home. Circumstances beyond his control prevented his taking up residence. And anyway, it sounds an unlikely story—though Dr. Johnson, Sir Joshua Reynolds, Garrick and the Emperor Napoleon III were among visitors who remarked on its beauty; and Napoleon, strolling captive on the deck of the *Bellerophon*, also admired it on his way to a less desirable situation on St. Helena.

Mount Edgcumbe was the only great Cornish house to be bombed during the Second World War; it was gutted, although a few years ago it was rebuilt with octagonal rather than the original slender round towers. The grounds remain as beautiful as ever—a favourite spot for an excursion from Plymouth, across the little bouncing Cremyll Ferry. There are English, Italian and French gardens, a nice little folly, a sheltered seat with grand Tuscan columns and a pediment, and a garden house built in the eighteenth century.

The nearest crossing to Devon, by car, is at Torpoint; and on the way to the ferry, which grinds its way over on chains, is the entrance to Anthony, an early eighteenth-century mansion, and the home of the Carew family. They lived at Anthony long before the present house was built, and nothing remains of the mansion in which Richard, the author of the *Survey of Cornwall*, lived once.

Richard was born in the old house in 1555; when he was 11, three years after his father's death, he was sent to Christ Church, Oxford, and by the time he was 19 he was at Clements Inn. But he decided to make a full-time career of running the Anthony estates, and settled in at home to become the best kind of civilised country gentleman of his age. His son described him in a memoir:

'My father took all the care he could to have me bred up in learning, well knowing the value thereof by the sweet fruits he still gathered of his own, which he always increased by his (almost incredible) continual labour; for without a teacher he learned the Greek, Dutch, French, Spanish and Italian tongues.... He ever delighted so much in reading ... for if he had none other hindrance, going or riding he would ever have a book and be reading.'

When he was 24, having spent Twelfth Night at a friend's house, he called on his way home at Trerice, near Newquay, where he met the daughter of the house, a 14-year-old beauty, Juliana Arundell. Some months later, he married her. Within a few years he had become not only a Justice, but Sheriff of Cornwall, and his travels about the county made him thoroughly familiar with it—so that when his friend (and contemporary at Oxford) William Camden, about to publish his own great *Brittania*, suggested he should compile a survey of Cornwall, he set about it with enthusiasm.

He wrote the book between 1585 and 1594: partial, lively, witty, it is and is likely to remain the best-written and in many ways the most revealing book that has ever been written about the county. It is not only a topographical survey, with descriptions of the great houses and the little farms, but it is a social survey too; Carew set down the remembrances and legends of the oldest inhabitants, notes on their dialect, their habits, their 'life-style', their temperament. The *Survey of Cornwall* is a lovely book: a fount of information about Elizabethan England, and a classic of its kind.

Carew did not write only one book: there are several poems, including a translation of Tasso's *Jerusalem*; an amusing satire, *A Herring's Tail*, and several essays, including *The Excellency of the*

English Tongue, which contains one of the earliest written tributes to Shakespeare.

As well as author and poet, Carew was a man of action: Colonel of the troops which protected the Tamar estuary against invasion at the time of the Armada. Everything about him promises that he was a truly endearing, pleasant, gentle man. He loved fishing, and built a saltwater pool on the shore of the little river Lynher, which he stocked with fish. There he would walk with his friends, of an evening, knocking on a stone with his stick to watch his fish come and be fed, thus 'confirming Pliny's assertion that fishes do hear'. He celebrated his pool in a set of verses:

> *I wait not at the lawyer's gates,*
> *Nor shoulder climbers down the stairs;*
> *I vaunt not manhood by debates,*
> *I envy not the miser's fears;*
> > *But mean in state and calm in sprite,*
> > *My fishful pool is my delight.*

Alas, nothing remains now of the fishful pool but traces of the banks, once surrounded by a palisade to keep out marauding otters. And Carew's original house has vanished, too, though some of the furniture and a little panelling remains in the present building.

Carew's grandsons became involved in the Civil War, on the republican side. John, the younger, was beheaded as a regicide (his signature appears on the King's death warrant); his elder brother, Sir Alexander, first joined the Roundheads and was Governor of St. Nicholas Island in Plymouth Sound (now Drake's Island). But he changed his views as the Civil War proceeded, and was beheaded by the Parliamentarians as a traitor. The Royalist Carews thereupon brought his crumpled portrait up from the cellars, where they had thrown it in disgust when he joined the enemy, and reinstated it, sewing it back into its frame with rough stitches which can still be seen.

Anthony is an interesting house—completed in 1721—with some nice family portraits, and the finest extant portrait of King Charles I: one of a number painted by Edward Bower from sketches made at the King's trial in Westminster Hall. There are four copies of this painting, all signed and dated 1648. By common consent, the Anthony copy is the finest, and all the tragic intensity of the King's ordeal shows in the noble bearing and dignity of his figure.

Torpoint Ferry was until a few years ago the only approach to Plymouth from Cornwall, and many hours have been spent sitting in sweltering queues for it. Torpoint was indeed traditionally too hot even for the Devil, who is said to have crossed into Cornwall by the Ferry route, but 'could not but observe that everything vegetable or animal was put by the Cornish people into a pie. He saw and heard of fishy pie, stargazey pie, conger pie, and, indeed, pies of all the fishes of the sea; of parsley pie, and herby pie, of lamy pie, and pies without number. Therefore, fearing that they might take a fancy to a devilly pie, he took himself back into Devonshire.'

A few miles up-river, is the much easier road bridge into Devonshire, running parallel to Brunel's great railway bridge of 1859. Brunel himself 'conducted' proceedings from a high platform as the huge first span swung into position in 1857; and 19 months later Prince Albert opened the bridge. A local ballad recorded the occasion:

> *From Saltash to St. Germans, Liskeard and St.*
> > *Austell,*
> *The county of Cornwall was all in a bustle;*
> *Prince Albert is coming, the people did say,*
> *To open the Bridge and the Cornish Railway.*
> *From Redruth and Camborne, St. Just in the West,*
> *The people did flock all dressed in their best.*
> *From all parts of England you'll now have a*
> > *chance*
> *To travel by steam right down to Penzance.*

When through carriages were inaugurated from Paddington to Penzance in 1867, the fastest train took 12 hours in each direction, and until 1869 third-class passengers (not allowed on the fast trains) took anything from 13 to 15 hours. The Flying Dutchman in 1871 still took ten hours, and until 1876 all passenger trains from Plymouth to Penzance stopped at all stations, so that it took 80 minutes to travel the 25 miles from Truro to Penzance!

But the achievement of taking the railway through to the west of Cornwall at all was a great one: the timber viaducts of Cornwall were justly famous—34 of them between Plymouth and Truro. Some of them had masonry supports (like the tallest, at St. Pinnock and Liskeard), but some—at St. Germans, for instance—were completely of wood, owing to the depth of the mud in the creeks they crossed. The railway still, today, runs through some lovely country—the Glyn Valley, between Liskeard and Lostwithiel, for instance.

Brunel, however, never made the journey, for by the time the Royal Albert Bridge was opened, he was dying; he was drawn across it, once, on a specially built platform truck, watching the great arches and girders pass slowly overhead. His career was at an end. Glance at his name, in huge gold letters at the Cornish end of his bridge, as you drive over the new road bridge which runs just up-stream of it, and think of him as you approach the toll-gate (a sort of customs-barrier) which passes you from Cornwall into Devon, and Plymouth.

CHAPTER FIVE

Plymouth and Dartmouth

Plymouth is a city with as proud and interesting a history as any other in the country. But in a sense the terrible blitz of March and April 1941 burned that history away: more than 80,000 buildings were damaged or destroyed. What city could hope to preserve its atmosphere through such an ordeal? That Plymouth succeeded to any extent is miraculous, and while practically nothing now remains of the place Drake and Raleigh and the Elizabethan adventurers knew, there are still corners of Plymouth where the past breathes strongly.

Much of the centre of the city is, of course, new: a visionary Lord Mayor—Lord Astor—conceived a Plan for Plymouth while the enemy bombs were still falling; and while subsequent planners have modified it, the spirit it put into the hearts of the Plymouthians led to speedy rebuilding after the war. St. Andrew's Church, built in the late fifteenth century, stood until the late 'forties with the word *Resurgam* painted on a board above the door which led into its roofless hulk; then was restored, with magnificent surety of touch. George VI laid a stone near the ruined Guildhall (perhaps less worthy of restoration, but nevertheless carefully restored), and from it the rebuilding of Plymouth continued, and continues still.

There has been much controversy during the process, as might be expected. During the 1950s it seemed that mediocrity might triumph; but then things improved, and while there is no outstanding modern architecture in the centre of the city, it has become a spirited commercial centre for Devon and Cornwall; and if one feels regret as a dusty line of cobbles becomes the only sign of another vanished street, one remembers too that Hitler's bombers destroyed much, much more than the City Council has subsequently disposed of. And a visit to the City Museum reveals that Victorian and Edwardian councillors, before Hitler (before the Kaiser, for that matter) also tore down much of the historical Plymouth.

Although man has lived in this area since he first began to walk on his hind legs (traces of pre-Ice Age man were found in a cave at Cattedown), it was not until the twelfth and thirteenth centuries that the city began to have any real importance—and then (as ever since) its importance was really as a place of war or preparation for war. In 1287, over 300 ships assembled in the Sound to go against Guienne; in 1355, the Black Prince sailed from Plymouth on his last campaign in France, and throughout the whole century the port was used for the trans-shipment of armies to and from France (and suffered accordingly). And of course in the most famous incident in the city's history (except perhaps for the departure of the Pilgrim Fathers), in 1588 the British Navy lay waiting for the approach of the Spanish Armada, with Drake engaged in his probably fictitious game of bowls below the walls of the fort which he was later to replace by a larger one, the true ancestor of the Royal Citadel.

The place of Plymouth in the history of the discovery of the New World was of the utmost importance. Drake sailed from the Sound in 1577 on his round-the-world voyage (how poignant was the moment when, almost 400 years later, Sir Francis Chichester returned from a similar one-man voyage, virtually at the same quayside!). In 1583 Sir Humphrey Gilbert sailed on his second colonising trip to America. And of course the Pilgrim Fathers (albeit accidentally, because of a storm) set foot in England for the last time, at Plymouth.

Strolling around the walls of the Citadel is as good an exercise as any during which to ruminate about Plymouth's place in the history of England. Looking out over the harbour, and then turning westward, one can plainly see how Plymouth's existence indeed depended on war—war on land as well as on sea.

The naval dockyard, the hospital, the victualling yard and the citadel itself, with the marine barracks and the Raglan barracks, are circled within the city by a series of outer forts which guard Plymouth and the neighbouring towns of Devonport and Stonehouse, now one city.

The city as a whole is a relatively modern conception. In the Middle Ages there was a series of small villages here; and even during the Elizabethan age the small townships maintained their separate identity. Between 1532 and the end of that century, Plymouth almost doubled in size. A whole new Elizabethan suburb grew up around the Barbican, and the town began to spread to the north as well (from the cluster of houses in the area where St. Andrew's Cross now whirls the traffic round).

But though most people think of Plymouth as an Elizabethan city (until 1941, that is), it owed its physical being, if not its historical form, to the years between 1810 and 1870, when the whole area between it and the Hoe was built upon, and when Union Street connected Plymouth and Stonehouse, and the centre of Devonport was designed and built.

In many ways those nineteenth-century architects and builders made the most of their splendid site: Plymouth, Stonehouse and Devonport lie marvellously situated on the hilly, rocky ground between the Tamar and Plym rivers—Hamoaze and Cattewater, as they become at their mouths. The Great Western Docks, Sutton Pool and Stonehouse Lake took advantage of the coves and creeks; Drake's Island lay in the Sound, convenient for defence and imprisonment; from the Hoe, the Citadel lowered protectively over the shipping; to the west Mount Edgcumbe provided as lovely a stretch of West Country landscape as any sailor could hope for who had spent long months away; while to the east the cliffs and rocks of Stadden Point and the Mewstone presented an implacable face to foes coming up-channel.

Such a natural theatre as The Hoe—the high ground commanding the Sound itself, and then dipping down to the north into the heart of Plymouth—must have attracted man's eye from the earliest times; and as the Roman sailors guided their ships towards Plymouth from Bordeaux, they would have glanced superstitiously up to where on that high ground two huge figures were outlined in white limestone. Gog and Magog, Plymouthians say; more likely Hercules, the Sun god, and some female earth goddess.

Later, the figures were erased; the village of Sutton cowered under the Hoe, anxious not to attract the attention of passing pirates. But by the time the ports around the area had become important, the Hoe's possibilities as a vantage-point and place of fortification had been thoroughly grasped. The City Arms show a castle with four towers: and this stood on the Hoe towards the end of the fourteenth century. Beside it, at High Cross, the Gog-Magog figures reappeared —freshly cut each year near St. Katherine's Chapel, where waits serenaded the Mayor and Corporation on Midsummer Night.

It was Drake who petitioned Queen Elizabeth for the provision of a really secure citadel on the commanding height of the Hoe, 'that the forces they allwaies have in readiness within said towne should be able to withstand the enemy if they were 5000 strong for 10 or 12 daies at the least without one penny charge to her Matie. In wch tyme the contrie might come to their reliefe.'

The appeal to the Queen's sense of economy was infallible, and building started. But it did not continue, and Drake's citadel was never really completed; in 1661 it was knocked down completely (apart from St. Katherine's Chapel, which presumably was within it) to make way for the present Royal Citadel.

The imposing main entrance is still referred to by Plymouthians as 'Wren's Gate', though it has been known for many years that it was designed in fact by Sir Thomas Fitz rather than by Sir Christopher. It is none the less handsome, as various visitors—from Charles II and his brother to Samuel Pepys, from bloody Judge Jeffreys to George III, from Nelson to George VI—have remarked.

The various buildings which huddle inside the walls are remarkably difficult for the amateur to date; built of the same stone and in roughly the same style, only one or two of them are obviously seventeenth century in origin. The Guard House and Governor's House are of good proportions but otherwise undistinguished; the Royal Chapel, on the site of St. Katherine's, has a nave built in 1668, and was enlarged in 1845. Its appeal is emotional rather than architectural.

The persistent visitor will still find Plymouth a place of interest, quite apart from its convenience as the largest conglomeration of shops and cinemas (no longer, alas, of theatres) in the West Country. There are still streets which it is interesting to explore, and the dockyards are still fascinating to those interested in maritime history. The Royal Naval Victualling Yard, designed and built in the 1820s by Sir John Rennie, covers 14 acres, so low to the water that many of the buildings stand on reclaimed land. There is a splendid gateway in Cremill Street with a 13-foot-tall statue of William IV on top, and with little carvings illustrating the work done inside the Yard.

William III presided over the foundation of the Royal Naval Dockyard on Bunker's Hill, which at first stood on four acres, but by 1765 (less than a century after opening) covered almost 70. 500 workmen ran it then; by 1800 there were over 1,000, and by 1910, 12,000. Now, there are 240 acres, including the 'new' yard at Keyham, opened in 1848 and twice enlarged, connected with the Bunker's Hill site by underground tunnel. Recently, the Yard has been considerably run down, and there is difficulty in discovering precisely how many men are employed there, much less how many are expected to be employed there in the next few decades.

Vanburgh himself designed the Gun Wharf, built in the 1720s, and among the felicities nearby is a delightful summer-house built during the reign of George III.

The churches of Plymouth remaining undamaged, or which have been restored since the war, are perhaps not outstanding; one brilliant stroke of imaginative planning preserved the shell of Charles Church—blitzed on the eve of its tercentenary in 1940—at the centre of a traffic island, as a memorial of the destruction the city suffered.

But an instantly recognisable historical landmark is now extremely rare in the centre of the city. In the main, the relics of the old city are stranded among much later buildings—like the Prysten House, just below St. Andrew's—or incorporated into them, like the Dominican Friary in Southside Street (founded in 1383), which has become part of a distillery.

If one had walked with Thomas Hardy the marble pavements of old Plymouth, one would have found at least considerable portions of it on which an overall pattern had been imposed; chiefly by John Foulston, a London architect who in 1811 won an open competition held by Plymouth Corporation for designs for a new hotel, assembly rooms and theatre. What a splendid group of buildings that was: the Royal Theatre with its great portico, next to it the Athenaeum, and nearby the Royal Hotel and Assembly Rooms. Old prints show the buildings at their best and most impressive. But the theatre was knocked down before the war to make way for an anonymously rectangular cinema; the hotel and assembly rooms went in the blitz, and the Athenaeum has been replaced by a modern hall. Foulston's Proprietory Library in Cornwall Street also vanished in 1941; a railway station replaced his Royal Union Baths as early as 1849; and much more recently the City Council disposed of St. Catherine's Church, the last notable example of the work of this great city planner in Plymouth.

Foulston's vision as an architect, if on the stolid side, was well-defined and clear. He came to live in Plymouth, and stayed for 40 years, during which time he built Union Street, Athenaeum Street, Lockyer Street, the Crescent, and most of the city's most elegant terraces. Nearby all the public buildings were his, and his personality dominated the nineteenth-century city; a mainly Greek taste, influenced by Nash.

He ventured outside Plymouth, too: to Devonport, where his extraordinary Town Hall (based on the Parthenon) still stands, with nearby the Civil and Military Library (this time in the Egyptian style), and Mount Zion Chapel (in the Mohammedan style, built for the Calvinists, and perhaps happily no longer with us). In the middle of it all, a huge column designed to uphold a statue of George IV, for which the money never became available.

The few remaining pieces of Foulston in Plymouth (unfortunately many, like the Crescent, looking sadly disoriented) are, one hopes, being cherished. The most undistinguished of buildings, if unique, assumes interest. This is rather what happened to 32, New Street, down near the Barbican, where there is a complete Elizabethan merchant's house—a good example of the many houses which must once have peppered this area. It stands opposite another Tudor house in a narrow street mainly of warehouses; the Old Plymouth Society rescued it from demolition in 1929, and keep it up well; there is a particularly nice staircase, constructed around a disused ship's mast.

Fairly recently, one has for the first time for many years been able to set foot on Drake's Island—originally St. Nicholas' Island. It was used as a state prison during the Civil War, and many republicans died on it, including General Lambert, condemned to death after the Restoration, but spared to pass the 16 long years of his imprisonment painting flowers and working out algebraic problems. Later, dissenting ministers were imprisoned here, denied even the comfort of the ancient chapel which had given the island its original name, but which was knocked down in 1548 to make way for extensive fortifications. The War Department held on to the island until recently; now there are Outward Bound courses there, and tourist trips.

Beyond the island lies the breakwater, two miles out from the Hoe, and built in 1812—a remarkable feat, with over four and a half million tons of limestone sunk to form its foundations. And further out still (but unmistakably part of the West Country scene), the Eddystone lighthouse, around which happy trippers were boated before the war, and occasionally, since. Smeaton's Tower, the third of the lighthouses to stand on the Eddystone rocks, was moved in 1882 when the rock on which it was perched began to topple, and stands now on the Hoe.

There is still much to be done in Plymouth: no one can spend long there without being surprised at the gaps which still remain in the overall city plan (they still remain in other war-damaged cities too; but somehow one expects more in Plymouth—for rebuilding there started with such panache and promptness). The muddled and hopelessly disorganised area north of the Hoe is perhaps the most urgent candidate for replanning. How strange so to neglect the approach to Plymouth's most attractive feature!

And then there is Union Street, planned by Foulston to connect Plymouth with Stonehouse, and between the wars as full of life and lusty vitality as, say, Soho. With over a hundred pubs splashed each side of the central Octagon, and with two theatres—the Palace and the Grand, complementing the Royal at the eastern end of the street —it was awash with sailors and adventurous civvies every night of the week, some of them attempting to match the record of a bo'sun who, sometime in 1923, allegedly managed a pint of beer in every pub in the street. Now, toothless gaps, occasionally half-stopped by totally featureless modern buildings, spoil Union Street; the Grand was damaged during the war and allowed to decay and ultimately vanish after it; the Palace, splendid in ginger majolica with *art nouveau* knobs on, is a bingo hall (while up on the Hoe, inexplicably, a concert room looking like an ambitious nissen hut is used for summer shows); Union Street is a nothing. Well, everything cannot be done at once; but one hopes that the City Council has some idea of what is to be done with the whole area from Union Street to the sea.

No one with a sense of history can walk the streets of Plymouth without seeing in the mind's eye the narrow-streeted Elizabethan town, with the merchant adventurers—tough as oak, and the same colour—striding before him down to their bobbing ships. William Hawkins was the father of the merchant trade in Plymouth: his son John sailed his father's ships from Plymouth to Spain and Guinea, and when he encountered the Portuguese slave traders, took a leaf from their book and carried on a thriving business selling human flesh and blood—with so little shame that his crest was a negro in chains.

The most famous of the merchant adventurers was, of course, Francis Drake, the slave-trading circumnavigating buccaneering little pirate of a man. He was born near Tavistock in 1541, in a farmhouse long since vanished. His house at the top of Looe Street, in Plymouth, where he lived when he was Mayor, has also vanished; but Buckland Abbey, where he lived as a landed gentleman during his frustrating years of rejection by Elizabeth, is now a showplace, administered by Plymouth City Council. It stands about six miles or so from the city, just off the main road to Tavistock.

Buckland is not simply *called* an Abbey; it *was* an abbey, founded in 1278 by Cistercians. The present house consists of nave and chancel, and looking at the outside of the tower, one can easily see the roof-line of the transepts and the thirteenth-century windows (now blocked up). In 1539, Abbot Toker surrendered the Abbey to Henry VIII, no doubt expecting the buildings to be wrecked, like so many other monastery buildings up and down the land. But Buckland was more fortunate. The King sold the Abbey to Sir Richard Grenville for £233 3s. 4d., and his heir, Roger, lived there—all too briefly, for in 1545 he went down with his ship, the *Mary Rose*, which capsized off Portsmouth in a mysterious and unexplained incident which drowned 500 men.

Roger's son was another Richard, now his grandfather's heir; and when he was eight, he succeeded to Buckland. He soldiered in Hungary and Ireland, and began to build himself 'a fair new house' within the walls of the ancient abbey. By 1576, he had finished, setting three floors within the church's great walls. At 34 he was a landowner and a born leader: yet forbidden to lead, for the Queen for some unknown reason delayed all his enterprises. In 1580, Drake sailed home from his voyage round the world—for the moment

England's and Elizabeth's greatest hero, but as far as Grenville was concerned, a vulgar upstart. He sold Buckland and packed his family off to his other family home at Stowe. Later, of course, he died in the heroic little *Revenge*, at Flores in the Azores. And Drake bought Buckland.

Though there is little physical evidence of his years there, the house remains more Drake's than Grenville's (in the way in which Chequers remains Churchill's rather than Macmillan's or Wilson's or Heath's). His famous drum, with his sword, and the gifts he received from the Queen, lie here; and it is easy enough to feel his presence through them. Powerful men leave powerful traces.

One of Drake's most remarkable and foresighted enterprises was the provision of a water supply which ensured Plymouth (and the fleet) fresh water for three centuries afterwards. From Meavy weir, near Sheepstor, he cut a leat which carried the water 17 miles to the heart of the city. This was in 1560, and it is still possible to follow the leat-line, here and there, for miles.

It was, I suspect, Drake's only real connection with Dartmoor. That great slab of rolling, wickedly unkind, bare land can have had little to commend it to a seaman. In its crueller moods it can seem, even today, as remote as the surface of the moon; there is even a resemblance between the moon-mountains and the bleak outcrops of rock at Saddle Tor or Great Mis Tor. Even when in the 1840s the railway reached Exeter, and in the '80s Princetown, the moor, retained its air of remoteness, and its designation in 1951 as a national park did nothing to tame it.

N. T. Carrington, a Victorian poet whose poem about Dartmoor ran into several editions, saw it as a desert:

> *Nothing that has life*
> *Is visible;—no solitary flock*
> *At will wide ranging through the silent moor,*
> *Breaks the deep-felt monotony.*

One knows that mood, certainly. But ravens, buzzards, rooks, crows, kestrels sweep across the landscape nevertheless; there is generally some movement somewhere—the occasional fox (there are many more of them about than one is likely to see); badgers and visiting otters; weasels and long-tailed field-mice. Tufted duck, pochard, mallard, goldeneye, have all come to the reservoirs at Burrator and Fernworthy, and naturalists have noted 75 breeding species and 41 non-breeding species of birds near Postbridge. There is life on Dartmoor, all right—there is also death as motorists, tearing much too fast along the A384, run down the occasional sheep, cow, or pony.

As with Bodmin Moor or the highlands of West Penwith, there are traces of man on Dartmoor from almost unimaginably ancient times. A few clues have pointed unmistakably to the presence, if only occasionally, of hunters, even during the Great Ice Age 17,000 years ago; and man was certainly living on the north-east hills of the moor at the end of the Mesolithic period (from the end of the Ice Age until about 3,500 B.C.). From this time onwards, Dartmoor has never been completely deserted.

From Saxon times, civilisation beginning to tame and soften him, man preferred to leave the windy surface of the high moor itself, and to live instead around the edges, in villages more substantially built than the rough settlements of his ancestors. Some of the villages around the moor are unmistakably built on Saxon foundations. Other Saxon villages lie under the earth, long since deserted and ruined, their outlines dimly decipherable.

The men who lived in them were not only farmers, of course. Tin was mined on the moor in 1156, and in 1195 the industry was in such a healthy state that 254 thousand-weight of tin was sent out to Richard the Lionheart at La Rochelle, so that he could adulterate the coinage with which he paid his troops.

Lead was mined at Marytavy and Bridestowe; iron at Haytor; copper at Sticklepath, Ashburton, Buckfastleigh. But if mining and farming were the moor's two favourite occupations, there were still others. Wool from the tough little Dartmoor sheep ('gross and stubborn', said a Florentine buyer in the fifteenth century) in the good years rivalled tin in importance as an export. There were corn mills, paper mills, flour mills; and at Cherrybrook, gunpowder was made to supply granite and slate quarries with blasting material.

There were quarries all over Dartmoor: some very small indeed, one or two really large. Dartmoor granite was used to rebuild London Bridge in 1825 (and now, presumably, withstands the heat of the sun in central Arizona), and of course it faced the sheer walls of Dartmoor Prison. Merivale, near Princetown, still supplies granite for buildings all over the country.

And finally, there was and is peat, the Dartmoor coal. The tinners originally had the exclusive right to cut peat on the moor, but in fact it supplied every household there with heat; enough for a fortnight's firing could be bought for a penny or twopence, even if one didn't cut it oneself. Nowadays it is scarcely used, yet the tangy smell and clear burning of a peat fire is not to be despised.

Farming is still probably the most important occupation of the moorsmen, and of course the most ancient. Livestock is the prime source of income; there is little to be said in favour of any other form of farming on such ungrateful land. Cattle, sheep and ponies graze on the open common; and are often of a traditional Dartmoor stock. The pony of course is a particular feature of the moor.

The Dartmoor pony is the direct descendant of the ancient breed of rough English pony that no doubt drew the war chariot of Boadicea. The ponies began to be exploited in the nineteenth century, not only for working in the coal mines, but for drawing governess-carts and costers' carts, and simply as presents for children: pretty little rocking-horse ponies, yet tough as they come. Now, they are rather more sophisticated—in demand abroad, and even considered for registration in the Stud Book. No wonder they are popular: too popular, in some ways. Visitors draw up by the roadside in their cars to feed the attractive little beasts, tempt them to consider the road exclusively a source of titbits, and place them advantageously for some more impatient motorist to run down. The sight of a maimed and dying Dartmoor pony is not a pleasant one.

The moor is, I suppose, as tame now as it has ever been or is ever likely to be. The Romans seem to have made no real effort to make it accessible by road; most of the early tracks and roadways date from Saxon times, and these were made permanent, or decayed, became more or less used, over the centuries. Clapper bridges bestrode the streams and rivers (and were not all ancient: one was built as recently as 1780, over the North Teign). Turnpike roads at the end of the eighteenth century greatly improved access to the moor and travel across it, and after the coming of the motor-car, surfacing, the building of new bridges, and the widening of many roads made it possible for motorists to penetrate to the wildest and previously most inaccessible parts of Dartmoor.

There was also a little rash of tramways and railways during the railway age, most of which have now completely vanished—including the little branch line to Princetown from Plymouth, which opened in 1883. At first there were three trains a day in each direction. But the loss during the opening year was over £500, and by 1889 with an average loss of almost £1,000 a year, the directors (noting sadly that 'the traffic connected with the Prison Establishment is not what might be expected'), resigned. As lately as 1955 it was possible to travel to Princetown by rail, and a pretty line it was. But the railway then joined the Cann Quarry Branch, the Lee Moor Tramway, the Haytor Granite Railway (with granite rails over which trundled heavy wagons carrying the huge blocks for the building of London Bridge), and the Newton and Moretonhampstead Railway, in oblivion.

Of all the developments which attempted to make practical use of the moor, and which succeeded or failed in various degrees, the most extraordinary monument to man's practical common sense (meaning either his caution or his inhumanity) was the building of the prison at Princetown, 1,430 feet above sea level, exposed to every wind that blows, and as nearly as possible in the dead centre of the moor.

The enterprise began with Thomas Tyrwhitt, an auditor to the Duchy of Cornwall, who bought some land at Two Bridges, and became seized by an insatiable appetite for Improvement. He improved the road from Dousland to Two Bridges, and then led it on to a little settlement he constructed on the highest nearby ground: an inn, a few scattered cottages, and eventually a new house. He called the house Tor Royal, and the settlement Prince's Town—in honour of his friend the Prince of Wales.

In 1805, the Government (and the people of Plymouth) was beginning to be seriously alarmed at the large number of French prisoners-of-war rotting in old hulks in the Hamoaze. Tyrwhitt saw the opportunity of using convict labour to continue his improvements at Princetown, and began pulling strings at court. On March 20, 1806, he laid the foundation stone of a prison near his house.

(Strange that anyone should want to lay the foundation stone of a prison!)

However desirable it may be to have a prison as remote from any sign of civilisation as possible, the problems of building at Prince-town proved formidable. David Livingstone, the architect, planned a stolid building within a 30-acre circle, wings radiating like the spokes of a wheel from a central hall. Cast-iron pillars were to support the hammocks in which the prisoners slept. But one after another, a stream of contractors went bankrupt as weather and transport difficulties made costs soar. But in 1809 the prisoners—5,000 of them—marched up from Plymouth. They were soon joined by 4,000 others, and the overcrowding was such that they were always on the edge of riot (and were at least once fired on by guards).

Tyrwhitt, by now a knight, continued to enlarge his village by establishing a market, a brewery, a corn mill, and many more houses. But he had not foreseen the fact that the French war would not last for ever; and by 1817 (one is happy to report) the last of the prisoners had been repatriated, and grass grew in the streets of Princetown.

Depressed, Tyrwhitt came up with another idea: why not scour the streets of London for poor children, remove them from their 'profligate associates' in the slums, carry them off to Princetown, and there give them religious instruction while teaching them to dress flax? No one but Tyrwhitt, oddly, thought this a very good idea. A few years later, he sold Tor Royal, went abroad, and died.

The prison stood empty for almost 30 years, although some of the buildings were used by a firm converting peat into naphtha. Then, in 1849, the Government decided to 'modernise' them, and use them for convicts. Princetown came to life again, and so did the prison (if life is indeed the word). Visitors occasionally draw up their cars, at a safe distance, and stare down at those forbidding walls. Dartmoor prison looks as attractive from this side of the walls as it must from the other.

It is impossible in a short section of one book to give a real idea of the Dartmoor National Park: it covers, after all, some 350 square miles, and is by no means as uniform in landscape as the word 'moorland' might lead one to suppose. Many visitors fail to realise, for instance, just how much beautiful woodland there is on the moor: in fact it was a royal forest as long ago as the thirteenth century, with boundaries set in 1240, when 12 knights walked around them; those boundaries remain the same 700 years later. The forests were spoiled over the centuries, and no serious attempts at planting were made until Tyrwhitt began work at Tor Royal, setting out among the local conifers patches of Scots pine, Norway spruce and European larch; he also planted oak, beech and sycamore.

The Duchy of Cornwall established a plantation of conifers at Brimpts in 1862, and just after the First World War the Prince of Wales ordered the planting out of 5,000 acres of moor to help replace the timber used during the conflict. By the end of the Second World War, there were plantations at Fernworthy, Frenchbeer, Bellever and Beardown, where Sitka spruce were planted which have now, after only 30 years or so, grown tall and stately, over five feet across the trunks.

Now, within the triangle formed by Chagford, Two Bridges and Dartmeet, are three really beautiful little forests: Bellever, Fernworthy and Soussons. Between Buckland and Buckfastleigh are others, some of them on private land. The Council for the Preservation of Rural England, keeping a wary eye on the essential characteristics of the moor, was in touch with the Forestry Commission as early as 1934, making sure that too much of the open land was not afforested; and the result is that co-operation between the two bodies has brought a tact in landscape planning scarcely equalled anywhere else in the West Country. Even the prehistoric sites have in a sense benefited, for though in earlier years many of them were indiscriminately destroyed by over-planting, now they are carefully preserved and set within the unfamiliar landscape in which they find themselves.

All over the moor are to be found the deserted villages of prehistory: Assycombe Hill, Cranbrook Castle, Grimspound (a Bronze Age village with walls still standing, and door-lintels and jambs still in place); Merrivale, Shuggledon, Whittor, Butter Hill, Dendles Waste, Trowlesworthy and Yes Tor Bottom ...

Many visitors to Dartmoor will keep their eye strictly on Widecombe-in-the-Moor, and make straight for it; it is of course celebrated for its song:

Tom Pearce, Tom Pearce, lend me thy grey mare
(All along, down along, out along lea)
Fer I wants to go to Widecombe fair
  Wi' Bill Brewer, Jan Stewer, Peter Gurney,
    Peter Davy, Dan'l Whiddon, 'Arry 'Awkes,
  Ol' Uncle Tom Cobleigh an' all ...

Widecombe's old church (dedicated, oddly, to St. Pancras—though I suppose the oddity is only comparative) forms an unselfconsciously lovely picture set against the village square with its elm, its old Church House, and its Glebe House. The church tower is the pride of the village, strong and elegant, carrying proudly a dignity which would make itself at home anywhere, but seems particularly suitable to the strength of the countryside which is its setting.

Dartmoor has not attracted a great flow of literature, and certainly no single novel as notable as, say, *Lorna Doone* or *Tess*; and of the good books set on Dartmoor or in the West Country generally, many (even such recent ones as Jack Clemo's novel *Wilding Graft*, about the clayland of Cornwall) are out of print. Some librarians, however, can still dig up a copy of R. D. Blackmore's *Christowell*, containing perhaps the best description of Dartmoor yet written. Eden Phillpotts' *Children of the Mist, The River*, and *The Portreeve* also admirable as sketches of Dartmoor life, and Henry Williamson's *Life in a Devon Village* and *Tales of a Devon Village* capture the atmosphere as well as any.

Visitors to Dartmoor should not, by the way, be under the illusion that the term 'national park' implies complete freedom of access, though Wordsworth's original conception (of 'a national property in which every man has a right and an interest who has an eye to perceive and a heart to enjoy'), suggests it. 43 square miles of the park are used for military training, and although no heavy artillery is used, the Royal Marines, regular Army, Territorials and cadets, helped by the Royal Navy and the R.A.F., do from time to time let off rifles, machine-guns, grenades, anti-tank guns and light field guns. There have been fatal accidents.

The moorland used for training is divided into three sections: the Okehampton range to the north, the Merrivale range to the south, and the Willsworthy range to the west. In the east of the moor about a third of a square mile of moorland is used exclusively for small arms firing.

The Army points out that it advertises times of firing in all local newspapers, and that men with binoculars keep an eye open for anyone wandering into the line of fire (firing a shot across his bows?). Red flags are flown from flagpoles, and at night red lights are shown; when these are displayed it is, to say the least, unwise to cross the boundaries of the training areas, which are marked with red and white posts. No firing takes place at Easter, August, or Spring bank holiday weekends.

Well, the Army must train somewhere. But in the middle of a National Park? And apart from the danger, military vehicles inevitably churn up the moorland; old rough tracks have been tarmacked; helicopters grind and growl overhead....

Dartmoor is skirted by two main roads: the A30 runs around the moor to the north, from Exeter to Okehampton and on to Launceston; the easier A38 to Ashburton and along the southern edge of the moor through Buckfastleigh to Plymouth. This road has improved beyond measure during the past ten years, and the traffic jams which once distinguished it have now almost vanished. Coming out of Plymouth eastward, the first traffic jam invariably occurred at Plympton St. Mary (the northernmost of the two Plymptons). A new by-pass now loops past the little town barely two miles from the centre of Plymouth, but once greatly its superior. In the Middle Ages, the presence at Plympton not only of a Priory but a Castle gave it greater prominence than Sutton, the scattering of buildings eventually to grow into the new city of Plymouth.

Plympton Priory was founded early in the twelfth century for the Augustinian Canons, and became within a hundred years the richest monastic house in the country next to that at Tavistock. The Castle was built at about the same time as the foundation of the Priory, by Richard de Redvers, Earl of Devon. It can scarcely even be called a ruin, now, although a few lengths of keep wall stand ten or 15 feet above ground on the hill above the town. The Priory buildings are in little better repair: a Norman gateway still stands, with little columns set in it, and with the wedges of stone above, in different shades of colour. A tower lifts its head above the gate, the windows in it originally in the undercroft below the refectory.

16 *St. Peter's, Meavy*

But both the refectory and the kitchen, which still stood a century ago, have vanished, their stonework no doubt pillaged and put into use elsewhere in one or other of the Plymptons, and no one has done much work on the original layout of the buildings.

It is worth walking down the narrow main street of Plympton St. Maurice, if only to experience the peace of it: even when main-road traffic ground its way up the main shopping street of the other Plympton, half a mile to the north, the main street of the older town was by-passed, and one could stroll relatively undisturbed by cars, and look up at the beautiful solid little Guildhall, built in 1690 with its entrance overhung by an arcade, a present from the town's two leading families, the Trubys and the Strodes. Further down the street is the Grammar School, which opened its doors in 1664, paid for by an owner of Fardel Manor, the home of the Raleigh family.

A little more than half-a-century after the school opened, through its doors walked its most distinguished pupil, and a son of its master: Joshua Reynolds. Samuel Reynolds intended his son for a doctor, but young Joshua's opinion of classical learning can be gauged from a very early Latin exercise of his which has survived. The exercise is not particularly well done, but the drawing of a bookcase made on the reverse, is. His father wrote under the drawing: 'Done by Joshua out of pure idleness'!

To the schoolroom, too (which still survives, with the cloister outside it) came Haydon, Eastlake and Northcote: Devon produced a remarkable little clutch of artists at roughly the same period. Northcote was a pupil of Reynolds; Haydon a pupil of Northcote. Though Reynolds was unquestionably the finest painter of them all, Northcote was perhaps in a way the more interesting man (as Hazlitt's records of his *Conversations* shows). He had a mordant if opaque wit. Haydon remembered going to him with a letter of introduction. Northcote looked sharply at the young man:

'I remember yeer vather, and yeer grandvather tu', he said. 'He used to peinte.' 'So I have heard, Sir.' 'Ees; he peinted an Elephant once for a Tiger, and he asked my vather what colour the indzide of's ears was, and my vather told un reddish and your grandvather went home and peinted un a vine vermilion.' Not perhaps the welcome the student expected, which may partly explain his later

17 St. Andrew's, Cullompton: south aisle

envious tattle about his master. But Hazlitt saw Northcote's true value: a noble old man, he said—'puts one in mind of a Roman Cardinal or a Spanish Inquisitioner'.

Plympton never took much notice of its painting sons, and takes little enough notice now. Reynolds' home was pulled down a century ago, and only a memorial in the church (Reynolds lies in St. Paul's, of course) recalls him.

Traces of the Trubys and the Strodes can be found still at Plympton. Sir George Truby, a Chief Justice of England in 1692, built himself a mansion behind Plympton St. Maurice Church; though all the passer-by can now see of his pleasant William-and-Mary building is its high stone garden walls. In Plympton St. Mary Church (which stood in the old Abbey churchyard—Plympton St. Maurice Church, the parish church, is a much less interesting building) lie many of the Strodes: Richard, who died in 1464, under a tomb with stone mourners miraculously whole even after the vandalism of the Reformation; and Sir William, who kneels between two wives, each leaning her cheek upon her hand.

Fardel Manor, where lived the founder of Plympton Grammar School, is about a mile from Cornwood, farther east along the A38. Fardel was a Saxon estate, and the manor is in Domesday Book. It is difficult to date specific parts of the house and its various outbuildings (including a chapel, one of the few remaining of the 300 or so private chapels Devon once possessed); but presumably most of the old part of the house is of the fifteenth century. In the fourteenth century the Raleighs acquired the estate by marriage, and it was thought for some time that Sir Walter was born here. In fact he was born at East Budleigh, where his father was living at the time with a third wife. But Walter certainly visited Fardel, and no doubt as a boy played around the large piece of stone which in 1860 was recognised to bear an Ogham inscription—the oldest form of Goidelic, devised in the south-west of Ireland in the fifth century. The Fardel Stone, removed from the Manor to the British Museum, was the first scrap of Ogham discovered in England, and the first to prove the presence of the Irish in the West Country as early as 600 A.D.

Fardel remains in private hands; until recently somewhat neglected, but recently refurbished, and the worst anomalies removed.

It is a splendid example of a small, stout family house of the fifteenth-sixteenth centuries, showing all the signs of an organic growth which added to the structure in the same way in which experience is added to a life.

A more sophisticated 'great house' is the one which Sir Joshua Reynolds knew well, and which he visited many times during his greatest years—both as friend and professional painter. Saltram, now the western headquarters of the National Trust, is the largest house in the county. John Parker bought a tumbledown Tudor manor in 1712, and built in its place a fine mansion, with the saloon and dining-room designed, with all that is in them by Robert Adam. Though it looks a little dull from outside, the moment one steps in under the dome which covers the entrance hall and staircase, one is in a comfortable home which is also a show-place. There is a fine collection of domestic furniture, and as one might expect, some good Reynolds', and a discriminating collection of Italian paintings as well.

The land to the west of Plymouth, a triangle between that city, Torquay, and Salcombe, containing Dartmouth, is a satisfying area for a holiday; without containing any houses as notable as Saltram, it has numberless little villages which—like Holbeton, Aveton Gifford, East Prawle—are worth a visit and afternoon tea.

From Plymouth, one can take a steamer for a couple of hours to bob around past the Mew Stone and into Wembury Bay, and then a little way up the Yealm, through steep hills overhung with trees, between Noss Mayo and Newton Ferrers. These two little villages have been for centuries commuter towns for the wealthier inhabitants of Plymouth, some of whom have more recently built houses of unimaginable vulgarity (or individuality, perhaps). An exception is Puslinch, built for the Yonge family in the early eighteenth century, apparently by a Plymouth builder who had been feeding on Wren: a very respectable imitation with, not far away, the fifteenth-century manor in which the Yonges lived before moving house.

Newton church is old, but rather dull; Noss church new, but rather dull. However, just over a mile to the east along the cliff from Noss is that community's old church, built presumably as much as a landmark for shipping as for worship. At the end of the last century the whole building became too dangerous for parishioners, and was given over to wind and birds; it is one of the most beautiful ecclesiastical ruins I know, even including the classical Abbey ruins—hanging over the slate cliffs of Stoke Point, its fourteenth-century walls are as much a part of the landscape as the rest of the magnificent scenery of this part of the coast.

The segment of country 'behind' Newton and Noss is 'old country', much used by the gentry of the twelfth century and even earlier; within the parish of Brixton alone are eight estates mentioned in Domesday Book. Not far along the road, much later, lived Old Mother Hubbard, whose house is still pointed out to visitors. She was housekeeper at Kitley House, and in its regency library is the only known first edition of her *Rhymes*, published in 1805. The housekeeper was probably only the Old Mother Hubbard who made the collection; the old lady of the rhyme itself must have been of a much earlier time—at least Elizabethan, for the third verse of her original rhyme runs

> She went to the joiner's
> To buy him a coffin,
> But when she came back
> The poor dog was laughing.

The rhyme of *coffin/loffin* is found also in Shakespeare.

Kitley is near Yealmpton, on the River Yealm, with its astonishing Victorian church (by Butterfield), the walls a mass of local polished stones, with black and grey marble pillars; so that one is surprised to find a brass memorial to a Sir John Crocker who died in 1508. What can he think of Mr. Butterfield's goings-on?

Holbeton, just south of the A379 (Plymouth-Kingsbridge) road a little farther east, is a lovely little village almost totally unspoiled. Follow the river Erme to the sea, and you find Mothecombe, a popular beach. Many handsome houses in the area, including Flete ('done up' handsomely by Norman Shaw), Mothecombe House, Membland and Pamflete.

Along the coast past Bigbury (a riot of tasteless bungalows), Thurleston (probably the prettiest village on the south Devon coast, named after a Saxon *thirled* or pierced stone, mentioned in a document of 845) and through Malborough, one comes to Salcombe. All this sounds easy : in fact, the area is unquestionably one of the most difficult tracts of country open to motor navigation! The shortest distance between two points seems frequently almost illimitable, and between Bantham and Salcombe, for five miles or so, there are almost 30 little stretches of cobwebbed road, running parallel at right angles to the coast, in which it is possible to ramble infuriatingly but happily for hours. Happily, because this is a very beautiful piece of West Country.

If, instead of passing through Malborough on the A381 to Sal-combe, one turns down a minor road to the little village of Hope, one can walk along the cliffs from nearby Bolt Tail to Bolt Head, four miles away at the mouth of Kingsbridge estuary. National Trust land, most of it (like so much West Country coastal land) and quite breathtaking. (Your breath may be literally taken if you attempt any climbing here; there have been several clifftop rescues.)

Salcombe is a pretty little village, sheltered within the estuary, and with nothing much going on except fishing and sailing. At the head of the estuary is Kingsbridge, the tower of St. Edmund's church standing sternly on powerful thirteenth-century arches. Its spire was a landmark for ships coming up the estuary—but not to Kings-bridge itself, which has never been a port, though it has a Promenade (with a house in which John Wolcot, or Peter Pindar, was born, about whom I have already written on page 53). Thomas Cookworthy, the great porcelain-maker and discoverer of china clay was born here, too.

Inside the church is a rather splendid monument (to a Mrs. Frances Schutz Drury) designed by John Flaxman, that enormously well-known and popular English sculptor and friend of William Blake, whose carvings are scattered all over England, but sparingly here in the west. This one shows a rather generously proportioned lady, a baby clutching at her skirts, while above her is another well-proportioned lady either standing on a set of concealed steps or ascending into heaven. The piece is peculiar in its narrative, and not perhaps one of Flaxman's happiest conceptions (though beautifully modelled, as usual). I prefer, as a memorial, the set of verses near the grave of an anonymous gentleman a little way off:

Here lie I at the chancel door,
Here I lie because I'm poor.
The further in the more you'll pay;
Here I lie as warm as they.

The A379 which leads from Kingsbridge across to Dartmouth is a rewarding road to take, especially as a means of sliding off southwards into the rectangle of land which lies between it and the sea. The spectacular cliffs between the Bolts are mirrored here on each side of Prawle Point, the most southerly piece of land in Devonshire. The hard rocks near the surface of the land fall away often into deep valleys and combes, many of them lovely green channels which are a pleasure during the heat of summer. They lie in the parish of Chivelstone, where there is a fifteenth-century slate church dedicated (uniquely in all England) to St. Silvester.

At Torcross, the A379 turns north and almost disappears into the sea: in fact in storms, this has literally been known. The road runs along the beach, and unwary motorists can occasionally be seen placing their summer blazers under the spinning rear wheels of their cars, having unwisely driven on to the sand for a few minutes' rest.

Up a brisk hill, through Stoke Fleming and past Blackpool Cove (where the men of Dartmoor thrashed an invading Breton force in 1404, causing Henry IV to order a *Te Deum* to be sung at Westminster)—and suddenly one is gliding down into Dartmouth under the Castle, and on to the quay. The original settlement of Townstall lies still 400 feet above the Dart estuary; now, Townstall and the later Dartmouth are one, the houses hanging one above each other down the hill to the waterfront in an impressive cascade. The town is a fitting key to the estuary itself, which, becoming the River Dart and running up to Totnes, provides a scenic river trip only equalled by the Cornish River Fal.

Dartmouth's position is such that its connection with the Navy was inevitable: on these waters floated the fleets which sailed off on the Second and Third Crusades, and Smith Street originally vibrated to ringing anvils as the hammers of the smiths beat out metal to repair the king's ships.

At the time of the Crusades, Smith Street formed the waterfront; but in the sixteenth century reclamation forced it inland—it and St. Saviour's Church, against whose very churchyard walls the ships once lay at anchor. (St. Petrock's church, within the precincts of the castle, is now more a seaman's church—at least by position.)

Land reclamation, and the growth of the town, followed its increasing importance from the time when Henry II, on his marriage in 1152, made trade with the south-west provinces of France possible. Out sailed the ships with cloth from Totnes; back with wine from France and Spain. Chaucer came here as a civil servant, and met the great local trader John Hawley, the Shipman of *Canterbury Tales*.

In the sixteenth century there was renewed prosperity as a result of the growth of the Newfoundland fishing trade: many new buildings were set up, and some can still be seen on the waterfront and nearby. But after the end of the seventeenth century, when the Newfoundland trade failed, and when the relatively dangerous narrow entrance to the harbour prompted the Navy to concentrate on Plymouth rather than Dartmouth as the focus of its preparations against the French, the town dwindled in importance. When the railway came west, it failed to come to Dartmouth, and the town suffered accordingly. Now only the presence of the Royal Naval College gives it still an air of mild prosperity.

But if Dartmouth is no longer in any real sense an important town, it is certainly an extremely pleasant and interesting one; not only physically, but historically. Its military defences are fascinating, and date back to 1388, when, it is recorded, the people were building 'a fortalice by the sea at the entrance of that port for the defence of the town and of the ships of other parts of the realm which touch there'. A wall and part of a tower of the fortalice still survive; but it does not seem to have been in use for long. The gentlemen of the area relied rather on erecting a few gun-platforms on their private houses—until 1481 or so, when the Castle was begun which still stands guard over the town, and which was the first castle in England designed with artillery as its main *raison d'être*.

During the early fifteenth century, the town had been guarded simply by a chain stretched across the harbour mouth—as at Fowey; and indeed there seems reason to suspect that Dartmouth's first chain was in fact stolen from Fowey! Edward IV seems to have been interested in the possibility of building a castle at Dartmouth, and granted £60 a year for five years towards its cost. Henry VII followed this up with a grant of £40 a year for the Castle's maintenance: a sum which was paid until the nineteenth century.

The building seems to have taken about 15 years: good employment for the dozen or so masons (at sevenpence a day) and for the labourers (fivepence a day). Down the coast by boat came the stone, and the giant beams (13s. 4d. was paid for the master-beam of the great tower).

The new artillery-minded architect set properly raked gun-ports in the thick walls, to cover the harbour—right down near the waterline, with garrison-rooms overhead. The ports were at floor level, for at this time guns were still laid on the floor for firing, and not mounted on wheels as they were when Henry VII built the forts at Falmouth 50 years later.

Defences did not stop with the completion of the Castle. In 1545 a gun-battery was set up on the cliff above the present bathing beach; there was a small castle across the estuary at Kingswear, and a little fort at Bayard's Cove (pressed into use again in 1940 as a machine-gun post, but abandoned because of the restricted field of fire it offered—precisely the reason why its use was discontinued in the sixteenth century!)

Dartmouth was a short-lived Royalist stronghold during the Civil War; Fairfax easily overcame an incompetent defence force and took town and Castle. And from that time until this (with the exception of occasional militia activities during the Napoleonic War, and the placing of a 4.7-inch gun there in 1940) the Castle has been dedicated to romance rather than action.

Delightful though Dartmouth still is, other delights have vanished: in 1864, making a new main road out of the town, planners demolished the Guildhall, once the medieval home of Chaucer's Shipman, and the seventeenth-century house where Thomas Newcomen worked on his plans for an engine run by steam: he was really the earliest original thinker in this line, and the least credited.

CHAPTER SIX

South Devon

Across the ferry from Dartmouth, and through Kingswear (as exposed to the elements as Dartmouth is protected—so much so that the iron guns in the fort there had to be replaced by brass ones, because of rust!), one can motor on to Brixham, a little fishing port with a ravishing view over Tor Bay, where in the nineteenth century the *Bellerophon* lay at anchor with Napoleon a prisoner on board. Earlier, Drake had sailed into the same bay with the *Capitane* his prisoner; the first prize he took from the Armada—so quickly that he was able to sink other Spanish ships with the prize's own guns and ammunition.

It was at Brixham, which has had its own moments of history, that William of Orange landed to end the Stuart dynasty and bring Protestantism back to Court; big-booted and muffled in rather undistinguished clothes, he stands still in statue on the quay.

Brixham has always made its living from the sea: making nets, using them in fishing, and building its own boats (and more recently, other people's). In the middle of the nineteenth century there were over 250 fishing vessels clustered in the harbour, manned by 1,500 men. But the fishing industry's collapse had its effect, and now the town is mainly concerned with the holiday trade.

It is a splendid place for a holiday, especially for walkers: the limestone cliffs spread high and wide from Berry Head right around the coast past Sharkham Point and Scabbacombe Head to the mouth of the Dart, over five miles away—and right at the highest point of Berry Head is an early Iron Age cliff-fort, cheek-by-jowl with the later (much later) Napoleonic Fort; when the latter was built, many Roman coins were found in the earthworks and ramparts on whose foundations it was set. From this point man has peered anxiously out to sea for many centuries; in a limestone cave not far away the bones of palaeolithic man spoke of the earliest inhabitants of Brixham, long before the Saxon settlement was set upon the site of St. Mary's

Church, on the open hill above the port.

Across Tor Bay, Torquay and Paignton are virtually one town, although they would no doubt deny it, and there are indeed what might be called tonal differences between them.

Paignton is the older of the two, but Torquay, which became in the nineteenth century 'the Queen of watering-places' and 'the Montpellier of England' is the more successful and popular, and has been since the 1840s. The Napoleonic Wars should be remembered here, for they made Torquay; they brought the British Fleet to anchor in the Bay—and with it came the wives and families of the officers, who found lodgings in the houses clustered around the minute quay which Torre Abbey had built 300 years earlier.

The visitors found the place extremely healthy; and no doubt told their friends about it. The word got around, and the town soon acquired a reputation for the kindness of its climate. Doctors began sending their patients there for the winter—to Plymouth by coach, then on by steamship down the coast. Between 1820 and 1840 the population trebled, and the town became a thriving and growing community. It was to Torquay in 1834-41 that Elizabeth Barrett Browning came, for her health's sake, and lived at Bath House by the harbour (now an hotel). At Babbacombe Bay, nearby, her brother was drowned—a tragedy whose horror remained with her for the rest of her life.

By the end of the nineteenth century, the population of Torquay stood at about 21,000; and the suddenness of its growth resulted, as it so often does, in a beautiful organic unity of town planning, under the watchful eye especially of two local families, the Carys and the Palks. Sir Lawrence Palk built the Royal Hotel ('for the reception of families of the first distinction'), and supervised the building of many terraces separated by open parks—Higher Terrace, Vaughan Parade, Beacon Terrace ... all easy on the eye, and all typical of the best nineteenth-century taste.

In the cemetery at Torquay lies Philip Gosse, the miniature painter unforgettably drawn at full length in the famous (in its day, notorious) *Father and Son*, first published anonymously in 1907. But, as is true of that other great father in modern literature, Sir George Sitwell, the portrait Edmund Gosse drew of his father somewhat diminishes him. If he was impossible as a parent, he had great virtues as a man. He came to Marychurch when he was 42, and began a study of the life of the Devon sea-shore which lasted until his death. He collected marine animals, and kept them alive longer than anyone else had succeeded in doing; and with a devotion which equalled that of Jonathan Couch of Polperro, he drew over 700 of them, setting the drawings out in his *Manual of Marine Zoology*, a masterpiece of its kind. Devoted until the last, he spent a cold night out with his telescope when he was 77, caught bronchitis, and died.

Strolling around Torquay, especially perhaps on a sunny spring or autumn day, one feels very close to the leisuredly Victorian spirit. In high summer it is a very different matter—the elderly gentlefolk who prefer the town cannot afford high season charges. But off-season, there seems very little distance between the quiet days of the 1880s, when consumptives coughed discreetly in the shelters along the front, and the hotels and boarding-houses were full of the less robust.... On the whole, the town still handles its holiday traffic with great tact; it is perhaps the most pleasant, if also the best-known, of Devon holiday resorts.

Torre Abbey, which founded the original hamlet in 1196, still survives in a range of buildings including a gatehouse, a magnificent tithe barn (124 feet long), an Abbot's Tower ... and in the outlines of the huge Abbey Church, with vast blocks of masonry lying within them, about the lidless coffin of the son of the founder, William de Brewer.

Paignton, right within the arms of the bay with Brixham at one extremity and Torquay at the other, rose to prosperity at the coat-tails of its neighbour. An ancient village founded by the Saxons, it had by the thirteenth century become a thriving farming parish with a market and a three-day fair; and became famous for cabbages and cider: the cabbages were large and sweet, and the cider sweet and strong, sent in great barrels up to Exeter, Bristol and London.

The town began to expand at about the turn of the century, after Torquay had more or less reached a comfortable size; perhaps it always attracted a slightly less pretentious type of visitor, and certainly relied on its reputation as a 'bathing place' as well as 'a place of resort for invalids'.

The one house of continual and fascinating interest in Paignton is Oldway, a mansion built in 1900, its façade splattered with Corinthian pilasters, and with clusters of giant Corinthian columns at its centre; on the sea side, Ionic columns quite as big. Inside, a really vast marble staircase sweeps up under a skylight and ceiling paintings to a marble gallery. Here Paris Singer, the American sewing-machine millionaire, brought Isadora Duncan, his mistress. He had the house built to his own designs, inspired by a single (and, one is tempted to suppose, speedy) visit to Versailles. Like many millionaires' quirks, Oldway is the kind of nightmare which is strangely attractive.

Supposing that one is staying at Brixham and visiting Torquay and Paignton (a desirable state of affairs, on the whole), one can also spend a day on the river Dart, hiring a boat perhaps either at Dartmouth or Kingswear, and chugging (rather than rowing) gently up to Dittisham for lunch. A lovely little Devon village, surrounded by plum orchards, with a little slate church with a red sandstone font, and (oddly) Pugin aisle windows; and nearby several small but attractive manor and farm houses—Bozomzeal, Downton, Lapthorne and Capton. Here, too, is a housing estate designed and built in 1937 by the designer of Welwyn Garden City!

After lunch, back into the boat, and farther up the most lovely of rivers to Stoke Gabriel, where the Dart salmon fishing industry thrives. Sandridge, a great house built by Nash in 1805, presides brokenly over a run-down but beautiful park. At Sandridge Barton, a farmhouse below the mansion walls, John Davis, one of the greatest of Elizabethan navigators and explorers was born, who first visited unknown arctic waters (narrowly missing discovering Hudson's Bay), discovered the Falkland Islands, commanded the ship which took Raleigh to Cadiz and the Azores in 1596-7, and took the *Black Dog* against the Armada. Almost as far from Stoke Gabriel as it was possible to get, he died a sad but typical death at the hands of Japanese pirates off Sumatra in 1605; another of the great Devon Elizabethan litter of sea-dogs.

He is one of the lesser-known of his breed, because he lacked any capacity for self-advertisement; but he was perhaps the most scientific of all the great Elizabethan explorers, and not without vision and imagination, as his surviving prose reveals; he describes, for instance, the voyage in 1585 during which he came to Greenland:

'The loathsome view of the shore and irksome noise of the ice was such as that it bred strange conceits among us, so that we supposed the place to be waste and void of any sensible or vegetable creatures, whereupon I called the same Desolation ... [but] the people of the country, having espied our ships, came down unto us in their canoes, and holding up their right hand to the sun and crying "yliaout", would strike their breasts: we doing the like the people came aboard our ships, men of good stature, unbearded, small-eyed and of tractable conditions....'

Above Stoke Gabriel one may reject river travel in favour of road, if only in order to make one's way through perhaps the most beautiful, lush parish in the area—Cornworthy. The whole landscape around the village is captivating, rich dark earth and rich green fields; and then there is St. Peter's Church, which was built in the fifteenth century, but refurbished in 1820, with beautiful results: for here is Georgian at its happiest—box-pews and panelled walls, with window-seats; a pulpit with a sounding-board; eighteenth-century brass candelabra, and clear glass windows. The Rev. Charles Baxter was Vicar while the restoration was going on; indeed, he was Vicar for 71 years—an unrivalled tenancy. No wonder he stayed.

At Ashprington, a little nearer Totnes, the countryside remains fairytale; and nature is improved by art, for Capability Brown laid out the grounds of the Sharpham Estate—many beautiful trees (including the largest recorded cork tree in the country); flowering shrubs and herbaceous borders, and beautiful walks. Captain Philemon Brown built Sharpham House; or began to build it. He had made £65,000 out of a single prize captured in the 1760s, and much of it went on the house, designed by Sir Robert Taylor, sometime President of the R.I.B.A., and a man who in this instance was un-typically lacking in discrimination. Captain Brown was killed in 1780, the house unfinished. It was, however, completed later, doing less than justice to its setting.

But now to Totnes, a small but fascinating town, dominated by its castle, atop a mount set up by Judhael, one of the leaders of the Norman campaign in the west. A Breton, he was exiled by William Rufus; but came back later to fresh manors and wider lands in the West Country.

The castle, a perfect example of a circular keep, has had its ups and downs; in the reign of King John, someone built a cob-walled house on top of the motte, and soon afterwards someone else built a hall in the bailey below, with Purbeck marble fittings and a slate roof. Very grand. But it was not used for long, and the castle itself is now very plain, though well-preserved.

Totnes was a busy little market town in Judhael's time; by Henry VII's reign it was second only to Exeter in prosperity; and it was not until the eighteenth century that its decline began. A decline however which is only relative : Totnes is a lively town still, with a bacon factory and a cider factory, and many thriving small businesses.

A walk from the bridge at the east end of the town to Fore Street is full of interest, with many nice nineteenth-century houses, and one more than nice eighteenth-century house, the King Edward VI Grammar School. But it is perhaps not so much the individual houses as their total aspect which is memorable : in some intangible way, they work together to make a pretty and (to use Prof. Pevsner's word) 'reasonable' setting. A happy town. Remember, while passing through The Plains (a beautiful square) William John Wills, who was born here, and went out as surveyor and astronomical observer on Burke's famous horse-and-camel expedition across Australia in 1860. All its members died on the return journey.

Not far from Totnes, just off the A384 on the way to Buckfastleigh, is Dartington Hall, on an estate which was the seat of the Duke of Exeter in the fourteenth century. The range of medieval buildings which remains is the most elaborate and beautiful in the county, and forms a remarkable whole with the tactful additions made by various landowners from that day to this : by, for instance, Sir Arthur Champernowne, an early member of the family which owned Dartington Hall until early this century.

The really fortunate thing about Dartington is that just at a time when the family fortunes were failing, and parts of the Hall beginning, quite literally, to totter, a wealthy American couple—Mr. and Mrs. Elmhirst—bought it and its lands, and launched there an elaborate experiment in the possibilities of running an old-style rural estate. A Trust makes use of the most modern scientific methods of farming and rural industry : it has set up a sawmill, a building firm, a model farm, a textile mill, a pottery making the most elegant glass —even an electrical firm to provide power. And, of course, there is Dartington School, in its time a very daring radical educational centre, only rivalled, it may be, by A. S. Neill's Summerhill; the cause of considerable scandal and discussion in Devonshire before the War, and even now from time to time the centre of contention.

The most notable event of Dartington's year, culturally at least, is the annual summer school of music, organised for some years now by John Amis: musicians—composers and performers—from all over the world come here to give concerts and recitals, to lecture and teach, in surroundings which are ideal for community living. To attend a concert in the Great Hall, with the musicians on the platform in front of the huge fireplace dominated by the White Hart of Richard II, is a quite remarkable and unique experience.

Outside the Hall lies the big open quadrangle, with the west block at one side of it—the original little manor house, with a gateway cut through it. Then there is the barn, now with a first floor, but with the lovely old roof still surviving; a range of buildings with little rooms reached by outside stairways; a five-storey tower which looks, even if it is not, wholly Tudor; and to the west, the gardens with their open-air theatre, presided over by one of Henry Moore's most placid, commanding reclining figures.

On the other side of Totnes, about two miles from the town, is the most romantic ruin in Devon: of Berry Pomeroy Castle, where the two great families of the area lived—the de Pomerais, who held the estate from 1066 until 1548, building one castle there in the early fourteenth century, and the Seymours. The son of Lord Protector Seymour built the second castle here in the sixteenth century; in St. Mary's Church nearby his giant tomb stands, with effigies rising one above the other, propped on their elbows in a rather superior manner, the uppermost clasping his staff at an equivocal but determined angle, and with the Protector's grandson, his wife, and a babe in a cot; then there is another little girl in an upright chair, and five sons and four daughters in ruffs, kneeling below the tomb.

The gatehouse, fourteenth century and really massive, leads into a narrow courtyard, faced by the ruins of the sixteenth-century castle, with its long hall. The front of the ruins, facing the courtyard, looks Victorian, but in fact is firmly sixteenth century, with plain mullioned windows. The castle is said to have cost over £20,000 in the sixteenth century, but was never completely finished. The family was very heavily fined during the Civil War (its members were fevered Royalists), and perhaps this inhibited them from further work. Although Sir Edward Seymour entertained the Prince of Orange in great state in 1688, his son chose to live elsewhere, and the castle was already falling down by 1700.

'Old mortality, the ruins of forgotten times'—I suppose it is indeed in the idea of mortality that lies the appeal of a ruin; and in the romantic sense so strong in Jane Austen's Catherine Morland. Anyway, this place has all the necessary ingredients, including a surrounding wood (mainly of beeches), and even a stream rushing down a miniature gorge below a lake.

West of Dartington, the main road to London—the A38—in its newly enlarged grandeur, sweeps past St. George's Church, Dean Prior. And perhaps it is right to do so, for there is nothing remarkable about the church itself—except that for almost 30 years its Vicar was the poet Robert Herrick, who is buried in an unmarked grave in the churchyard.

One thinks of Herrick as the poet of the country—of flowers and harvest, trees and streams and country love. If one looks to him for pretty sets of verses on the delights of Devonshire, however, one is disappointed. Although he became fascinated with various aspects of country life, he never quite recovered from the shock of being removed from the sensual and intellectual delights of town to the remoteness and clodhoppery of the country. He hated Devonshire and its people:

> *Rockie thou art; and rockie we discover*
> *Thy men; and rockie are thy wayes all over ...*
>
> *A people currish; churlish as the seas;*
> *And rude (almost) as rudest savages.*

And again:

> *More discontents I never had*
> *Since I was born, than here,*
> *Where I have been, and still am sad,*
> *In this dull Devonshire ...*

18 *Fourteenth-century nave of the Cathedral of SS. Mary and Peter, Exeter*

A couple of miles farther along the trunk road, and one passes through the little village of Buckfastleigh. A mile off the road to the north, King Canute endowed an Abbey. It survived thrivingly for only 100 years, and although it was refounded in 1134 under the Cistercians, and became their most important western house, it went the way of the other English abbeys, and by the end of the eighteenth century a Gothic mansion had been built on part of its site.

But in 1882, French Benedictines from Pierre-qui-vire bought the house and the whole estate, and gradually ever since have been expanding the buildings. The work began under Boniface Natter, the first Abbot. But he was drowned as he set out in 1906 for a visit to the Argentine. A survivor of the shipwreck was Fr. Anscar Vonier, who was chosen to succeed Abbot Natter; and by any standards he was a great man. With a sovereign in his pocket, and a single helper who had been a mason, he began to rebuild the abbey church, and it was consecrated in 1932 by the Archbishop of Westminster. It follows the lines of the original church, with imitation Norman and imitation Gothic, and has a tower (finished in 1938) over the crossing. It is, alas, a tame building, though undoubtedly a fine achievement by the community ... and the enthusiasm and kindness of the monks, and their delight in showing one around, makes a visit a real pleasure.

Holne, up a little by-road north of Buckfast towards the edge of Dartmoor, is the village where Charles Kingsley was born—a little moorland village all in grey with nothing to dignify it except the name of its still well-known son. Kingsley was born in the Vicarage, still thatched, and in the middle of a field; faintly, if one listens, comes the sound of a stream (did the Water Babies live here?). Kingsley was the son of the Parson, so his time at Holne was short; the family soon moved to Northamptonshire, then to Clovelly, then to London; and eventually he became the Rector of Eversley in Hampshire. So Holne can claim, I suppose, little credit for the origin of *Alton Lock*, *Westward Ho!* and *The Water Babies*; or for the Christian Socialism which Kingsley preached throughout his life, and which made him one of the earliest and finest of radical clergymen. However, one might think of him while looking into the little church here, under the barrel roof where he was christened.

Ashburton, farther on the road to Exeter, is by-passed, and so remains largely unaffected by the worst incursions of twentieth-century traffic. Celia Fiennes called it 'a poor little town'. Well, maybe it is; but it is also graceful and charming, with a little main street ambling uphill and down, and everything discreet. Even The Hall, whose builder in 1803 placed prominent busts of Byron and Scott to impress visitors, avoids pretentiousness by some alchemy, and the Methodist Chapel with an outsize portico manages to sit happily in its setting. This is the kind of thing Devonshire gets away with, time and time again—but perhaps *time* is indeed the word, and we look more kindly on errors of taste because they are the errors of another age, and have anyway been outdone by more recent errors such as the Headmaster's House at Dartington, put up in 1935 in the modern style, and as utterly without reference to its setting as the 1971 motor car now sitting on the plains of the moon.

The A38 leads one on from Ashburton to Exeter, passing through Chudleigh; and two or three miles south of Ilsington, 500 feet up within reach of Hay Tor, on Dartmoor. This is a lovely, well-preserved village with neat old cottages; and in its church on April 12, 1586, was baptised John Ford, a nephew of Chief Justice Popham, who became an important dramatist. *'Tis Pity She's a Whore, The Ladies Triall, The Witch of Edmunton* were all important works, and Ford had a marvellous dense way with dramatic verse, and a quick eye for an effective image:

> *I am ... a mushroom*
> *On whom the dew of heaven drops now and then.*

He was a deeply melancholic man, as a contemporary's snapshot of him records:

> *Deep in a dump John Ford was alone got,*
> *With folded arms and melancholy hat.*

He returned to Devonshire in old age: but where he is buried (perhaps at Ilsington) is unknown.

The A38, as one follows it, passes through Chudleigh, which was almost entirely destroyed (like so many Devon villages and towns) by a voracious fire, in 1807; after which it was rebuilt and became quite large and prosperous because of the new traffic passing through it *en route* to Plymouth. I mention it mainly because of some nearby tracts of country: Chudleigh Rock, a limestone mountain, provides a good area for a ramble and picnic (indeed, in Victorian times many an excursion was made there); and just to the east is Ugbrooke, built in 1760 by Capability Brown, who also laid out the grounds. The Adam brothers decorated the interior of the house, which is not handsome, but in a lovely setting—and nearby, in a really beautiful and extensive park, is a grove of beech trees where Dryden is said to have had a favourite walk (he used to visit the first Lord Clifford here, staying in the old mansion which was replaced by the present building).

Before one reaches Chudleigh there is the chance to turn off either to right or left: the right turn offers Newton Abbot (mainly celebrated for its comfortless railway station), and the road goes on through Kingsteignton to Teignmouth. And Teignmouth really is a charming town. If Exmouth is the oldest resort in the county, Teignmouth follows it closely, for families began to come here for the summer as early as the middle of the eighteenth century. It had a fairly ordinary history until then, checkered by occasional visits from the French, who looked in from time to time to burn, pillage or bomb. But by 1803, it had become 'fashionable', and local landowners and builders began its expansion, building beautiful little terraces and streets, and constructing a grand impressive centrepiece in Den Crescent, with Assembly Rooms at its centre (now a cinema, but at least surviving). Here, too, was built a Library—Croydon's, in Regent Street—to which every morning for a while in the spring of 1818 came the slight figure of John Keats, then spending a holiday in Teignmouth, and sharing lodgings in The Strand with his brothers Tom and George.

Fortunately, there were plenty of dances and theatres to amuse him; for, as too often is the case in Devon in March and April, it rained almost continually during his stay, so that he found the county 'a splashy, rainy, misty, snowy, foggy, haily, floody, muddy, slipshod county—the hills are very beautiful when you get a sight of 'em—the Primroses are out, but then you are in—the cliffs are of a fine deep Colour, but then the Clouds are continually vieing with them'.

Devon men were 'the poorest creatures in England', Keats thought; but he took his usual lusty view of the girls, and wrote a happily erotic poem to a Devon maid he encountered on his way to Dawlish Fair. And it is difficult, if one loves Keats, not to see at Teignmouth (as Charles Causley did)

> *the crystal poet*
> *Leaning on the old sea-rail;*
> *In his breast lay death, the lover,*
> *In his head, the nightingale.*

Teignmouth has another rather sad literary memory: of Jane Austen, who came here in 1801 with her parents, and who according to her niece 'made acquaintance with a young clergyman then visiting his brother, who was one of the doctors of the town. He and Jane fell in love with each other, and when the Austens left he asked to be allowed to join them again further on in their tour, and the permission was given. But instead of his arriving as expected, they received a letter announcing his death.'

Jane returned to Teignmouth, and visited Dawlish too, from time to time; and Dickens was also attracted to Dawlish, and indeed made it Nicholas Nickleby's birthplace. It was almost equally popular with Teignmouth during the nineteenth century, and is still a pretty town, though the fact that Brunel took the railway brashly right across the strand between the town and the sea has not improved it (pleasant though this is for railway travellers).

Stonelands Gardens, laid out by Capability Brown and Humphry Repton around the house Nash designed for Sir John Rennie (the designer of London Bridge) are open to the public—informally beautiful, with rhododendrons, magnolias, cherries, maples, azaleas, and walks through woodlands by a river.

As the train passes along the coast from Teignmouth through Dawlish, it ducks under red sandstone cliffs between land and sea, passing weird knobs of red rock (one of which bears a distinct resemblance to Queen Victoria), and then follows the line of the Exe estuary towards Exeter. Halfway up the estuary it skirts the east side of Powderham Estate—a mild and gentle enclosure with grazing deer, and Powderham Castle watching them. Miss Austen, passing along the road to Exeter on the other side of the estate, must have seen it as a very desirable property.

It came into the Courtenay family in 1390, and has remained there —the Courtenays built a new aisle to Powderham Church in 1487, with the help of eightpence donated by the parishioners. The original castle was not a castle at all, but an Elizabethan manor house, its plan now obscured by bits and pieces added on in every century until the nineteenth, when some very strange shapes were superimposed on to the front of it. However, it must always have been a castle in intention: strongly fortified—so much so that the Royalists were able to hold out stoutly against Fairfax during the Civil War: though they surrendered at last. Architecturally, Powderham is undoubtedly a hodgepodge; but with some nice rooms inside, including a really very fine hallway with staircase, and a music room designed by James Wyatt, who had then recently finished building the famous Pantheon in Oxford Street, London.

In 1839, Charles Dickens, finally losing patience with his extraordinary, improvident, Mr. Micawber-like father John (who by that time was selling bits and pieces of his son's manuscripts around the streets of London in a vain attempt to raise money to pay his own debts), went secretly down to Devonshire to find a cottage to which he could exile his parents—for their own good. He found a six-roomed cottage and garden at Alphington, near Exeter, for £20 a year; took it; and moved his parents into it. 'I've settled the governor for life,' he said happily. Not so; John seems to have spent very little time at Alphington, popping up in Greenwich and the Isle of Man, full of vain schemes. But the Alphington house can still be seen, an unexpected association with the great novelist; and as a bonus, the church there has a very beautiful Norman font.

The semi-circle in which we have travelled from Ashburton around to the coast and up towards Exeter embraces perhaps the richest part of Devon as far as country landscape is concerned. Exmoor and North Devon, still to come, are colder and bleaker altogether. When people think of Devon, they think, I suspect, of the kind of landscape to be seen in the south—though it forms only a very small part of this third largest county in England.

One can return again and again to South Devon, with its coastline split by estuary after estuary—the Axe, the Otter, the Exe, Teign,

Dart and Yealm, the Plym, the Tavy and the Tamar. And inland between them lie so many attractive villages that it is impossible to list them all here. They reflect the mildness and richness of the country they lie in, with their cottages in red sandstone or cob, whitewashed or pastel-coloured, often with thick thatch (the shortage of thatchers resulted in some tiling of old roofs in the 1940s and 1950s, but now the old craft seems to be reviving, and perhaps the rot has been stopped—though thatching is expensive enough to persuade some cottagers to think about replacing their roofs. It may be that a local-authority grant should be made to retain thatch on presently thatched roofs.)

It is worth turning off a main road, in this area, at almost any opportunity, and ambling through the little villages—and there is the added advantage that the roads are wonderfully quiet in the by-lanes, even if the main roads are crammed. Stick a pin in the map at random anywhere around here, and one finds some village which will welcome one: Ashcombe, say—a tiny place under the shelter of the Great Haldon hills, four or five miles inland from Dawlish. Just an ordinary Devon village, but with some lovely little houses, including a beautiful pure early nineteenth-century verandahed vicarage, and a church with a Norman tower, with wagon roof and colourwashed walls—dedicated to St. Nectan, whoever he was. Well, if Ashcombe is not by any stretch of the imagination a village one would make a special detour to visit, neither is it a village one would ever regret having come across. Nor are, say, Dunscombe, Ideford, Mamhead (with one of the most beautiful Parks in Devon, with ravishing views from 800 feet up, out over the sea), and the others.

The whole Teign Valley, from Teignmouth right up to Doddiscombsleigh, is a very beautiful one, with lovely villages snuggling into the hills not far from the river. The riverside churches are particularly worth visiting. At Doddiscombsleigh itself the reason is the glass: made by Frenchmen, and almost completely fifteenth-century in origin—white and yellow, with plenty of plain glass still to give the church light and airiness. In the east window is a seated Christ (himself relatively modern), with the Seven Sacraments surrounding him: Eucharist, Marriage, Confirmation, Penance, Ordination, Baptism, Extreme Unction. The other windows, completely medieval, are the only examples of their kind in the county outside Exeter

Cathedral, and are very beautiful indeed. One of the workmen of Clayton & Bell, who did some restoration work in the eighteenth century, made a claim to posterity by scratching on the medieval figures: 'Coles glazier done this window March 1792 whom God preserve amen.'

Ashton, just downstream of Doddiscombsleigh, has St. Michael's, its font still capable of being locked against witches, and with a good Jacobean pulpit, fifteenth-century painted figures on the wainscoting of the rood screen, and some fifteenth-century glass as well. Dunchideock has a wonderful screen, too, and is perhaps the prettiest village in the river valley, with cottages clustering round the medieval church up on the slopes of Great Haldon. And at Brideford the rood screen, with little carved figures—apostles, saints, prophets—on it, once bore the initials of Katherine of Aragon and of Walter Southgate, the rector in 1508, who gave it.

Chagford, a village which lies six or seven miles west of Doddiscombsleigh, just off the A382 from Newton Abbot to Okehampton, is beautifully set on the edge of Dartmoor in perhaps the most lovely part of the Teign valley. It is beautiful in itself, too, with its crouching, ancient granite bridge; so is nearby Whiddon Park, near a small gorge; and all around, old farmhouses, very typical of the countryside in their grey sturdiness. But I think of Chagford always as the place where young Sidney Godolphin died—whose name, to the Royalists of the Civil War, was as memorable as those of Rupert Brooke, Wilfred Owen, or Julian Grenfell (in the First World War), or Alun Lewis or Sydney Keyes (in the Second). Indeed, Rupert Brooke is a good comparison: like Brooke, Godolphin showed early brilliance—he was M.P. for Helston when he was only 18, and his poems (though now long out of print) show the influence of Donne, though informed by a much lighter and more ethereal personality.

Godolphin, only 33, rode into Chagford one dark winter's morning in 1642 with a band of Royalist horsemen led by Sir John Berkeley. They had been pursuing retreating rebels from Okehampton towards Totnes; but did not know that Chagford had been occupied. Suddenly, there was a shot, and Godolphin fell from his horse, crying 'O God, I am hurt!' A musket ball had struck him just above the knee. Though a thatched inn is sometimes pointed out as the place where he died, contemporary accounts say that he died as he fell, of that rather eccentric wound.

Sir Bevil Grenville wrote: 'One losse we have sustained that is un-valluable, to wit Sidney Godolphin is slaine in the attempt, who was as gallant a gentleman as the world had'; while the historian of the Civil War, Clarendon, said of him: 'There was never so great a mind and spirit contained in so little room, so large an understanding and so unrestrained a fancy in so very small a body.'

It is still true, I think, as Clarendon put it, that Godolphin left 'the misfortune of his death upon a place which could never other-wise have had a mention in the world.'

Circling round the eastern edge of Dartmoor from Chagford, one reaches Okehampton, a quiet and unexceptional town, useful as a centre from which to explore the southern part of North Devon. But before this, as far as our present tour is concerned, we should perhaps return to south-west Devon, and fill in the land which stretches away north from Plymouth to the coast.

At Yelverton, the main road divides, the B3212 making east to-wards Princetown, the A386 north-west to Tavistock. But earlier, one may take one of the minor roads off to the east, through Meavy, to Sheepstor, where is Burrator Reservoir, a man-made lake the raw edges of which have softened in the 80 years since it was made, so that it now looks completely natural, the moorland planing down and becoming one with the water—beautiful in every weather, under the shelter of Sheep's Tor.

What an extraordinary place in which to find, beneath the walls of a stubby little fifteenth-century church, the tombs of two Rajahs! But here lie Sir James Brooke, first Rajah of Sarawak, and his nephew Sir Charles, the second Rajah. James was born in India, the son of a Devonshire serving soldier. He came home for his education, but was soon back in India as an infantry cadet. When his father died and he inherited a fortune, he showed some signs of becoming a layabout; he bought a yacht, and sailed idly off around the world, happening on Sarawak in 1839, when civil war was at its height. He helped to suppress the revolt, and was made ruler of the province—5,000 squares miles of it, complete with headhunters, and a population of 300,000 people of at least four nationalities.

He spent almost his entire fortune on Sarawak, while the British Government confined its energies to refusing him any kind of help.

He was constantly in the middle of the most histrionic adventures, on one occasion escaping from Chinese pirates by a spectacular night swim, before being rescued at the last moment by his nephew Charles and a band of equally piratical Malays.

Sir James died in 1868, and was brought back to Sheepstor, where he lies in the churchyard under a vast slab of Aberdeen granite. Sir Charles carried on as second Rajah, made Sarawak a British protectorate, and completed the process of civilisation his uncle had begun. Here was British empirical paternalism at its most striking. Sir Charles, too, returned to Dartmoor after his death in 1917; his memorial is of Dartmoor granite.

Inside the church is a memorial worth a glance: to Elizabeth Elford, who died in 1641, and lies on a couch, her baby at her side, three little daughters kneeling nearby, and the angel of death by the parted curtains above the bed. Simple and charming.

Now, on to Tavistock.

Like so many Devonshire towns, Tavistock as one sees it today is almost entirely nineteenth century—although the presence of tin not far beneath the surface of the land brought man to this site in prehistoric times, and there was a military post here a hundred years before the Conquest. The Abbey, the remains of which (few enough) lightly litter the ground to the north-west of the present church, was founded by Ordgar, a relative by marriage of Athelstan, the first King of all England. Sixteen years later it was destroyed by visiting Danes; but built again by Ordgar's son, governed the town until Henry viii broke it up in 1539.

More could be made of the ruins, if it were not for the buildings which have grown up on the site since: the Great Gate, for instance, lies in the present Vicarage garden; a piece of the Abbey wall has become part of the Bedford Hotel; the old Town Gate stands in the middle of the present town square. But it is worth looking carefully at these fragments, for they nurtured some notable men. Alfred, one of the Abbots, crowned William the Conqueror at Westminster on Christmas Day 1066; and the Abbey housed the earliest printing press in the West Country—and one of the earliest in Britain.

By the seventeenth century, the tin trade had been replaced by the cloth industry, which had been growing in importance for some time; the fifteenth-century church (to St. Eustace) reflects the town's growing prosperity. It is lofty and spacious, and its main glory is perhaps the tomb of Sir John Glanville: an alabaster carving of the knight, lying on his tomb, supporting himself on an elbow, his Judge's robes lying in folds along his body, and his hand resting on a skull. By his side kneel his wife, facing the altar, and (strangely separate) their five children, headless, alas.

The John Fytz memorial nearby is not nearly as good; though it has a macabre interest, for kneeling behind the tombs of his mother and father is the figure of Fytz's son, who murdered two men, and then nervously killed an innocent bystander who knocked at his door, before finally committing suicide.

Two main roads lead northward out of Tavistock, through the drizzle (usually; King Charles said there was only one thing certain in this world, and that was that it would be raining at Tavistock) either to Launceston, or over the moor to Okehampton. But of course there are many minor roads to the little villages nearby; Chaddlehanger and Marytavy and Quither.... This is the best way (if one doesn't mind the possibility of getting lost) to Lewtrenchard, with a pretty church in which there is a modern reconstruction screen with a loft containing 23 paintings of saints and scenes from Galilee, put up by the Vicar, the Rev. Sabine Baring-Gould, rector of the parish for 43 years, and a prolific writer on the West Country. He brought out two or three books during every year he lived here; and in them there is a wonderful collection of West Country legend. He died at the age of 90, and is buried in his church.

If it seems a little eccentric to be commending a country parson and amateur author, I might add that he also wrote some hymns, including *Now the day is over*, *Onward, Christian soldiers*, and *Through the night of doubt and sorrow*.

Lydford, five miles to the east, on the western edge of Dartmoor, was one of the four settlements in Devon chosen by King Alfred as a vantage-point from which to fight the Danes. It has never been a large town; but its importance was underlined when in 1195 a castle was built here in which to keep important prisoners—a bluff, square keep two storeys high, with windows for defence narrowing to a slit in the outside wall, looking out over a ravine in which runs the river Lyd. No doubt this was one of the most important towns in the county (and a large parish, too, with something like 50,000 acres of more or less wild countryside to cover).

During the reign of Ethelred ɪɪ and Edward the Confessor (in the eleventh century) coins were minted here, and the medieval town must have had considerable dignity. But by the end of that century Launceston had become the new military centre of the area, and Lydford's decline began. Only Charles Kingsley attempted to give it back a little importance by chronicling in *Westward Ho!* the history of Roger Rowle, a sort of Western Robin Hood. Today, few visitors to the west know the town; though it has a certain charm, and in the churchyard one of the most original epitaphs I know:

'Here lies in horizontal position the outside case of George Routleigh, watchmaker.

'Integrity was the mainspring and prudence the regulator of all the actions of his life. Human, generous and liberal, his hand never stopped till he had relieved distress. He had the art of disposing of his time so well that his hours glided away in one continual round of pleasure and delight till an unlucky minute put a period to his existence.

'Wound up in hope of being taken in hand by his Maker and being thoroughly cleaned and repaired and set going in the world to come....'

Northward again the land between Holsworthy and Okehampton is gently bleak: without the forcefulness of the Dartmoor landscape, yet without the richness of the south Devon countryside. The villages, too, tend to be open and guileless, and while here and there unexpected tidbits of history flash up to surprise one (who would have thought for instance that Henry de Bracton, the first great rationaliser of English law, in the fourteenth century, was born at the tiny village of Bratton Clovelly?) it would be silly to propose that this was the most interesting tract of Devonshire. Indeed, neither Holsworthy nor Okehampton themselves are particularly interesting, either—though near the latter is, next to Berry Pomeroy, my favourite ruin in the county: a fifteenth-century castle up above the West Okement River, with a grand Norman keep foursquare among the wooded hills.

This was one of the largest Devonshire castles, its kitchens equipped with two big ovens to feed its garrison (commanded by its builder, Baldwin de Brionys, made Earl of Devon in reward for his activities at the Battle of Hastings; what a giving-out of honours, what division of the country, was made after that battle!) Henry VIII took the castle to pieces, having confiscated its parkland; and the Courtenay family, who had acquired it in the thirteenth century, gave the remains to the town.

Again, northward through unexceptional countryside to the sea. It is difficult to be enthusiastic about this part of Devon: somehow, it is a nothing—without the harsh glamour of the moorland, and with villages almost without personality, very widely scattered, and (though each has its history) unremarkable. The difficulty I find myself in in describing this part of Devon, is not new : Thomas Westcote, Gent., who published the first really comprehensive modern topographical guide to Devonshire in 1630, found the same area barren of interest, and was reduced to examining in detail the pedigree of almost every single family, in order to fill out his narrative.

There is one family, however—or one family name—well worth recalling; in a little hamlet on the A386 from Hatherleigh to Great Torrington was born a Devonshire man who played a dramatic part in the Civil War. Merton itself is little more than a church (and a church so heavily restored that its original form is hardly discernible); but in the font of that church was baptised George Monk. Monk's family had lived in Great Potheridge, a manor house near the village, since the reign of Henry II at least. Monk himself, in later life, demolished the old house and built a mansion on its site. Later, this in turn was torn down, though the great oak staircase still survives.

Monk himself was born in 1608, and like many young Devon men had a taste for adventure; when he was 17 he sailed off to Cadiz with an expedition, and two years later served under the Duke of Buckingham. He had a distinguished army career for the next ten years, but when the time came threw in his lot with Cromwell, and served him loyally (oddly enough, at sea as well as on land; he was in command of the fleet which defeated the Dutch under Martin Tromp in 1653).

It was after Cromwell's death that he really became a man of enormous influence. He was an enthusiastic, determined and ruthless upholder of Parliamentary democracy; when there were signs that an ambitious clique of Army officers in London were about to seize power in 1659, he conducted a violent purge of his army, replacing almost overnight well over 100 officers and N.C.O.s whose politics or religion he mistrusted. Then he marched to London, defied the Rump Parliament and its determination to remain in control, and enabled the meeting of a full Parliament which recalled Charles II.

Monk was responsible, more than any other single man, for the Restoration being conducted without bloodshed; he had a wonderful instinct for knowing how public opinion was running, and relied on it. Charles II made him a knight of the Garter, and Duke of Albemarle, with a pension of £7,000 a year. In semi-retirement he came back to Merton, and built himself a grand house; bravely, he always made for London at the first sign of national trouble—even travelling to the city during the Great Plague and the Fire which followed it. He died in 1670. He was one of this country's most distinguished professional soldiers, a model of quiet reticence and determined control. His troops called him 'Black George' and adored him, though his discipline was exceptionally strict even for his time. His only son died childless, so the line became extinct; but he was one of the great men of Devon.

Nine or ten miles westward across rolling, sometimes wooded country, is another village: Bradford, which is notable only for the fact that Dunsland House stands nearby—Dunsland, held by the Bickford family from 1634 until 1817, and indeed held by inheritance (sometimes through the female line) from the time of the Norman Conquest until 1947. Originally, it was a small Tudor house, but in 1630 the Arscotts of Arscott remade it, and the Bickfords added the splendid north wing in the 1680s.

The rooms are spacious and of noble proportions, and the north wing has a plaster ceiling which is the glory of the whole area: immensely delicate moulding of flowers and garlands—and nearby a fireplace also carved with flowers, and with *putti* and wildfowl. Like so many other great houses, this one became very dowdy and brokendown during the Second World War, but has since been beautifully and carefully restored. It is a showpiece, and certainly should be seen.

On the north coast, Devon begins at Welcombe, which is not only barely the Devon side of the border, but really is almost wholly Cornish in flavour; some mistake, one is tempted to say, must have been made by the cartographers. Even the dedication of the church is to St. Necton, a saint well-known in Cornwall, if virtually nowhere else. The notable thing about Welcombe (apart from the beautiful and very early timber screen in the Church) is that it almost makes Cornwall an island, for the Tamar rises in the hills behind the village, traversing the whole of the county before reaching Plymouth Sound.

Another great Devon river, the Torridge, also rises nearby; it flows into its estuary only twenty miles or so away, but makes a considerable tour before doing so.

I suppose that it is not until one stands at Hartland Point that one really feels one is on the north coast of Devon rather than of Cornwall. From Hartland, 300 feet above the sea, one can look right across Barnstable (or if you like, Bideford) Bay to Baggy Point, or even Morte Point (fearful name) beyond. If one looks westward rather than eastward, one faces America, for 'the long swell from Labrador' theoretically breaks on the rocks of these tall cliffs. This is heartbreakingly beautiful country, and I am bound to say, devoted though I am to the north coast of Cornwall, that this stretch of cliff landscape probably beats it; as further west, buzzards slip through the almost always turbulent air, and the cries of the curlew are as common here as those of lesser birds elsewhere. No wonder passing seamen took stories of the coast back to Ptolemy, the great geographer, and that Hartland Point finds itself in his maps (as Hercules Promontory).

Five miles or so along the coast eastward from the Point is a village which is about as well-known for its picturesqueness as Polperro is in Cornwall. Clovelly is indeed unique: a village tumbling down a steep hill like a cataract, the cobbled 'main street' (and the quotation marks are essential!) so steep and narrow that donkeys are the common form of transport, towing after them a sort of Devonian droshky. The Lords of the Manor, the Hamlyn family, had for many years a completely autocratic command of the village; and one does not have to approve wholeheartedly of autocracy to realise that but for them it would not be nearly as unspoiled as it is. The miniature harbour at the bottom of the hill crooks a protective arm around a few rowing boats, and up on the hill above is Hobby Drive, a lovely three-mile wooded walk laid down by Sir James Hamlyn in the nineteenth century.

Clovelly must have been almost completely unknown until the middle of the sixteenth century, when a distinguished member of a local family, the Carys, built a strong pier and made the only safe harbour between Appledore to the east and Boscastle, over the border in Cornwall. But only the local herring fishermen took notice of the village, until in 1855 Charles Kingsley published *Westward Ho!* (his father had been rector of Clovelly from 1830 until 1836, and both the village and the Cary family figure in the book). Five years later Dickens wrote about the village in *A Message from the Sea* (that Christmas story starts with a description of the village, 'built sheer up the face of a steep and lofty cliff').

By 1895 there were three small hotels and a great rash of boarding-houses in Clovelly, and a local guide-book complained that its 'picturesqueness ... is not improved by the cards announcing "hot water for tea" and other refreshments which greet us at almost every step in the main causeway'. Far more visitors crowd that causeway now than climbed off the excursion steamers on to the little pier in the last century; but Clovelly survives them with remarkable grace, and it is impossible not to recommend any traveller to go there.

CHAPTER SEVEN

Exmoor and
Exeter

Of the sizable chunk of North Devon which lies east of Bideford (or Barnstaple) Bay, these two towns form the focal points, together with Ilfracombe. Historically, Bideford is to North Devon what Plymouth is to the south: Tennyson set the town into his narrative of *The Revenge*—and not arbitrarily, but because indeed it supplied sailors for the major expeditions of the Elizabethan adventurers, sailing with Raleigh and Drake, Hawkins and Frobisher and Grenville. Five ships set out from the Torridge estuary to fight the Armada; and Bideford men sailed off to colonise Virginia.

It is Charles Kingsley's town, of course—though he was born at Holne. He wrote most of *Westward Ho!* here, in a house which is now the Royal Hotel, but was once a sixteenth-century merchant's home. Down by the river in marble he still holds a pen and a book in his hand; fancifully, the book might contain his description of the town, 'beneath its soft Italian sky, fanned day and night by the fresh ocean breeze, which forbids alike the keen winter frosts and the fierce thunder heats of the midlands'.

Bideford bridge is justly famous: 24 arches stride across the Torridge, and have done so since the fifteenth century (though it was repaired, certainly, as recently as 1638, and then survived for another 230 years before needing to be widened). The original bridge of the fourteenth century was of wood, and when a fund was raised for a new bridge, rather more money came in than was needed—so the bridge fund built schools and allocated money to the town's poor.

Bideford church was rebuilt almost completely in 1864; but it still has its Norman font (where the first Red Indian ever brought to England is said to have been baptised!), and some of the old monu-

20 *Topsham: pre-Georgian house with Dutch gable*

ments—including one to Sir Thomas Graynflydd, who died in 1530, and was the grandfather of the immortal Grenville of the Revenge. His bones lie beneath the sea off Flores in the Azores, but his dying words are set out on the church wall. Tennyson, too, recorded them:

> *Sink me the ship, Master Gunner—sink her,*
> *split her in twain!*
> *Fall into the hands of God, not into the hands*
> *of Spain!*

It must be admitted that if Bideford has the history, Barnstable on the other hand has the personality. Bideford is a strangely anonymous place, without many interesting houses or public buildings. Barnstable is absolutely charming: mainly eighteenth century, restrained, polite, with poise and true gentility (though it, too, had a roistering past: matching Bideford with another five ships against the Armada).

There is no quay here now: just Queen Anne's Walk, a colonnade with Tuscan columns and a statue of the good Queen; but one can populate the place with ghosts, for here is where the quay *was*— here strode the old sea captains, and here too walked Samuel Pepys, courting the penniless Huguenot exile Elizabeth St. Michel, a 16-year-old girl who was to become his wife. Charles, Prince of Wales, came here when he was 15, during the Civil War, to be with Royalist friends. And, most celebrated but least documented event, it is said that Shakespeare appeared here in a play, with a touring company.

The church was tiresomely restored by Gilbert Scott in the 1870s, and one would not mention it at all were it not for a splendid collection of monuments, most of them to seventeenth-century merchants and their wives. Here, in frozen effigy, lie Elizabeth Delbridge, Raleigh Clapham and his children, George Peard, Richard Ferris, Nicholas Hake, Richard Jeable, Richard Harris, Frances Horwood (studiously leaning on a pile of books), and the rest. Nine-year-old Nicholas Blake stares blandly from under a canopy, with a bowl of bubbles nearby.

Barnstable bridge crosses the Taw, 13 of its 16 arches medieval; and some of the town's streets, too, retain a medieval atmosphere.

21 *Brendon Hills, Somerset*

Its most notable citizen was John Gay, the friend of Pope and Swift, Steele and Addison: as Pope said,

> *Of manners gentle, of affections mild,*
> *In wit a man, simplicity a child.*

And of course, the author of *The Beggar's Opera*, that smash hit of 1727. Gay left Barnstable, one gathers, as soon as he was able; his natural laziness perhaps did not commend him to the local people who knew him, and he was apprenticed to a London draper while he was in his teens. A sympathetic, jolly man: his first publication was a poem, *Wine*, denying the possibility of successful authorship to those who drank only water!

Between Bideford and Barnstable it is worth leaving the main road to reach Horwood, one of the most beautiful villages nearby: no distinguished architecture, but a village that is all of a piece, thick with the atmosphere of its placid history. Placid except for a memorable day when 10,000 Cornishmen led by Michael Joseph, the big blacksmith of Bodmin, marched through the village towards London to protest at Henry VII's exorbitant taxes. Joseph's horse lost a shoe at Horwood, and for centuries it was nailed to the door of the church. Now it has vanished. The rising itself came to a sick end in London, and Joseph was hung, drawn and quartered at Tyburn, 'taking pleasure upon the hurdle, as it seemeth by words that he uttered, to think that he should be famous in after-times'.

Four miles to the east, by minor roads twisting through rich fields, lies Tawstock; and in the churchyard one of the sweetest epitaphs in Devon—to poor little Samuel Kidwell, 11 months old:

> *He tasted of life's bitter cup,*
> *Refused to drink the potions up;*
> *But turned his little head aside,*
> *Disgusted with the taste—and died.*

Tawstock itself is a lovely village, with marvellous trees around it; and St. Peter's Church attracts anyone interested in ecclesiastical architecture, providing several problems of dating. It is a large building, and crammed with monuments, a vast number of them to the

Earls of Bath and their family. William Bourchier, the third earl, is particularly magnificent, his wife beside him in a glowing robe, and their four children with them. Lady Rachel in white marble is near a monumental tomb-chest borne on the backs of four seated dogs. The tomb-chest of Sir John Wray, who married a Bourchier in 1652, was only brought here from St Ive, near Callington, in 1924!

Tawstock Court, behind two thatched cottages, was burned down in 1787; only the gatehouse remains of the original Tudor mansion. The present house follows more or less the plan of the earlier one; but is largely Victorian Gothic.

North of Barnstable, across the head of land which the Taw estuary makes into almost a separate county, lies Ilfracombe, over-hung by Lantern Hill, where in Henry VIII's reign local penitents took turn and turn about to keep a light burning. Ilfracombe, formerly a tiny fishing village, became in Victorian times a popular seaside re-sort—and when the herrings ceased to grant a living to most of its population, Sea View and Bella Vista, and some larger hotels, took over. So the town is mainly nineteenth century, built up around a very few remaining earlier houses: the Victoria Pleasure Grounds, the Collingwood Hotel, and the Ilfracombe Hotel (now, with Gothic windows and French pavilion roof, the Municipal Offices), the Tunnel Baths and Bath Place all contribute to a rather pleasant *ambience* which is eminently and typically sea-sidey.

Apart from the various delightful old farmhouses lying in the hills between Ilfracombe and Barnstable (not, I may say, very perilous hills), there is little of great note to see in this happily un-sophisticated, undemanding countryside. Though it is perhaps worth following in the footsteps of St. Brannock to Braunton. That saint lies under the altar of his large and interesting church, which he built in the fifth century or so. At least, he began it then, having been instructed in a dream that he should build a church in the place where he met a sow and a litter of pigs. Having come over from Ireland via Brecknock, where he was tutor to the family of King Brychan, he eventually encountered his sow somewhere in the Braunton area, and his little chapel presumably became St. Brannock's Church. To prove it, high above the wide nave is a boss carved with the sow and her litter. West of the church the land falls away beyond the Great Field to Braunton Burrows, and shows the sea the way back to Ireland. The Great Field, within living memory, was divided still into over 90 strips, which were worked in the true old medieval fashion.

Following the coast from Ilfracombe eastwards through Paracombe (where in a fold in the hills St. Petroc built a cob-and-wattle chapel, later to become the present, almost disused, unrestored, plain church he dedicated to him, and saved by Ruskin from demolition) one begins to be conscious of a roughening of the country—of the proximity of the last of the great West Country moors, Exmoor. But first, here are Lynton and Lynmouth.

Lynmouth has by now almost totally recovered from the tragedy of 1952, when a sudden flood demolished much of the town, though scars can still be seen. Among the buildings destroyed then was the cottage which Shelley rented in the summer of 1812, with his wife Harriet and their strange friend Miss Hitchener. Shelley spent most of his time writing violent anti-government propaganda and sending it out bobbing in bottles from the coast, when, as he wrote in *Queen Mab* (which he began here)

> *those far clouds of feathery gold,*
> *Shaded with deepest purple, gleam*
> *Like islands on a dark blue sea.*

Dear, sweet Shelley, spending his evenings rolling copies of *The Devil's Walk* and cramming them into bottles, or constructing elaborate boats out of waterproofed wooden boxes to contain the lengthier, more ambitious *Declaration of Rights*. Or sending up balloons with little literary squibs attached to them, to sail over the hills and startle the Exmoor sheep.

Lynton, 500 feet up above its sister town, is dominated by still higher ground, a series of cliffs rolling up to 1,100 feet above the sea; and the two towns are connected by a hill, from which (an earlier guide-book relates) rival guest-house keepers looked out through telescopes for approaching visitors, descending on them with a most un-English clamour, to claim them for their own. The A39 on to Porlock and Minehead crosses into Somerset soon after ducking uphill through Countisbury, and edges between Exmoor and the sea. And Exmoor is in some ways perhaps the most compulsively interesting of all the West Country moors; despite its bleakness, its addicts are many, and return to it again and again.

Exmoor is not as rich in prehistoric remains as Dartmoor, or even the moors of Cornwall; partly, perhaps, because stone was not so readily available, and prehistoric man lived in huts whose walls were of turf, and vanished with their builders. There are, however, still some considerable monuments of man's persistence here: Chapman Barrows, for instance, on one of the moor's highest points, and with a nine-foot slate longstone nearby; the rough and enigmatic square of stones at Brenton Two Gates; the strange rows of stones at Brendon Common and Cheriton Ridge; or the triangle at Challacombe Common. Here and there, too, are iron age camps (Mounsey Castle and Brewer's Castle, for instance, between Hawkridge and Dulverton)—and two Roman sites have been excavated at Old Barrow and Martinhoe Beacon: signal stations and forts looking out over the Bristol Channel.

A Roman soldier stationed at Martinhoe between A.D. 50 and 75 must really have felt at the end of the civilised world. The damp rains and mists (Tacitus says) dismayed the soldiers more used to the blue skies of Rome. This was their westernmost venture into the West Country; and it lasted a comparatively short time. Then Exmoor was left to its wild self, the Dark Ages came, and there was silence until the coming of the Anglo-Saxons 200 years later.

But it was the Normans who really established the Exmoor forest, built one or two forts, and set up game preserves, in which 'the wolves and such like ravenous beasts being destroyed' (as an Elizabethan author wrote) 'the residue being beasts of pleasure as well as delicate meat, the kings of this land began to be careful for the preservation of them, and in order thereto to privilege certain woods and places so that no man may hurt or destroy them there; and thus the said places became Forests'.

The Wardens of Exmoor ruled the forest with a cruel law from 1204 until Edward IV removed their rulership by imposing his own. Poachers of the King's venison were liable to mutilation or death, and a Robin Hood who set up business in the area would have had plenty to do. In 1306, even an official ordinance admitted that the people 'are by the officers of our forests miserably oppressed, impoverished and troubled with divers wrongs, being everywhere molested'. But gradually the laws were relaxed and the borderers maintained their own right to holdings on the moor.

For a few years the moor passed out of the hands of the Crown, for in the year of the beheading of Charles I the freehold was sold to James Boevey, a rich merchant who retired from London to these Westward uplands, where he presumably had little need for the seven European languages he could command. His whole life, John Aubrey, that splendid gossip, said, 'has been perplexed in law-suits, which have made him expert in human affairs, in which he always overcame. He had many law-suits with powerful adversaries; one lasted eighteen years.' He built the first house in the forest—at Simonsbath, right in the middle of the moor; it still stands there, the date of its building, 1654, carved over a chimneybreast.

At the Restoration, while many Cavaliers almost starved, Boevey (a Vicar of Bray if ever there was one) lost the freehold of the moor, but contrived to lease it for a mere £46 13s. 4d., and planted an oak tree in celebration. He thrived in ownership; and when he died, his wife inherited the Wardenship, and exercised it until late in life.

In 1819, an Enclosure Act put an end to the Royal Forest; the land was put up for sale by tender, and a Mr. John Knight bought it for £50,000, moved into the house at Simonsbath, and set himself to make Exmoor bloom.

By 1824, Knight had built a wall around most of his property—nearly 30 miles of it—and had begun to improve the roads, and build a dam across the little river Barle to form Pinkworthy Pond, covering about seven acres, and almost 30 feet deep. Surely, though as pools go it is picturesque enough, Knight cannot have been exercising a yen for landscape improvement in so remote a spot? No one knows what the pool's purpose was, and Knight's papers do not tell us.

But if he was playing at landscape gardening at Pinkworthy, his plans for cultivating the moor were serious, and he began to exercise them; he ploughed in the Barle valley, he limed the ground, burned the rough grasses, and planted wheat and barley. The wind demolished both crops. He brought West Highland and Hereford bullocks to Exmoor : they attacked passers-by, so that several of them had to be shot; the remainder could not survive the winter without hay or corn.

Knight had a success with sheep, however : he introduced the

Cheviots which have done so well on the moor, and he improved and strengthened the native strains of Exmoor horses. And his son Frederick was perhaps even more successful in bringing prosperity to Exmoor; he made several separate farms, and found tenants for them. At first they found the going hard, and many failed; but eventually the battle was won, and both livestock and crops began to make sound profits. It is an extraordinary story of fortitude and persistence on the part of one family, and in very tough and ungiving country.

The most wonderful sight on Exmoor, and one which strikes into the memory so sharply that it will never be forgotten, is the sight of the great wild red deer—the largest of British wild mammals, with great horns spreading above his head and crowning a truly royal beast. There are about a thousand deer in the Exmoor national park at present, and herds of 30 of these ruddy brown animals moving solemnly across the moorland like a fleet of ships is an inspiriting one, but not common—the deer are not used to people, much less cars. You may see a herd by chance; but the only real way to ensure a sighting is to persuade someone who knows the moor well—and, more important, knows the deer's habits—to take you. Be prepared for a day, or perhaps two or three, of silent waiting. The boredom which is the price of the sight is well worth bearing.

The friendliness of Exmoor is not easy to define : indeed, it is perhaps not even a word that many people would use, for in winter the moor can be quite as severe as Dartmoor; and at the best time of the year is subject to sudden mists and damps. As the Forestry Commissioners put it in 1651, 'the said Chase is a Mountenous and cold ground much be Clouded with thick Foggs and Mists', while the annual rainfall can reach 80 inches! In the depths of winter the brisk winds which are almost always blowing can build up enormous snowdrifts, like that described in *Lorna Doone*, when 'there was nothing square or jagged left, there was nothing perpendicular; all the rugged lines were eased, and all the breaches smoothly filled.... Not a patch of grass was there, not a black branch of a tree; all was white; and the little river flowed beneath an arch of snow; if it managed to flow at all....'

But the moor in summer, and on bright days even in winter, can be a glitteringly beautiful place, with the sun striking colours of heather and gorse, and the mistier colours of the grasses. And it is quite possible to sit coatless in a sheltered corner of the highest part of the moor even in January; while in August the breezes are always there to cool the walker.

In 1689 the moor was reckoned 'a very barren place and very full of Bogges'. Somehow, these bogs seem to have dried up—even at Farley Water, where in the 1890s a horse was swallowed; there are no really dangerous mires now, although plenty of places where one can sink in over one's shoes: not difficulties one is likely to encounter if one sticks to the roads—and there are enough roads now to enable one to get a very good idea of the moor without stirring from the car. On the other hand, a real exploration of any area as wild and unspoiled as this had best be mounted on foot, and I doubt whether anyone would get the full flavour of, say, the Barle or Exe valleys from the roads that pass through them.

The part of Exmoor a great many visitors enquire for, then make for, is the Lorna Doone country—which properly speaking is the 25 square miles or so stretching inland from the coast between Foreland Point and Porlock Bay, as far as the road connecting Simonsbath and Exford—and in particular, the Badgworthy Valley. This is not the Doone Valley, however—that lies north of Hoccombe Water, at the back of Badgworthy Hill. Though, as usual where fiction is concerned, R. D. Blackmore always said that he 'romanced' the scenery as much as the characters. Still and all, he was fairly accurate, for Jan Ridd describes how his mother counted 14 one-roomed cottages at the Doone settlement; and a researcher has identified 14 ruined foundations in the Badgworthy Valley.

Blackmore seems certainly to have drawn on many legends of the Doones for his book—legends of a band of criminals who settled at Badgworthy in the 1620s, and laid many local farmhouses waste, leaving the dead and dying with the words

> If they ask who killèd thee,
> Say 'twas the Doones of Badgworthy.

But it was Blackmore who in 1869 made the family immortal, in the only one of his books to survive. And even those who have never read *Lorna Doone* and probably never will, seem to achieve some *frisson* of excitement by finding Doone Valley, and walking on the hills above Lorna's cottage.

Somerset makes a considerable incursion into Exmoor (which I continue to think of, perversely, as Devonian, though a good half of it must be in Somerset). For tidiness, then, let us retreat a little and look at the rest of Devonshire before returning to the north coast-line. Many of the towns and villages lying around the edges of the moor catch its mood, and remain proud and remote: like South Molton, high above the surrounding countryside, with its plain and stern church tower; North Molton, with a 100-foot high sandstone tower; Hampton, again with an uncompromising, no-nonsense tower.

Tiverton, south on the A396 from Hampton, is another matter: a really wonderful, richly decorated church introduces one to a town founded by the Saxons, and given a charter in the twelfth century. If its first few centuries of life were quietly agricultural, it became the most prosperous of all the Devonshire wool towns by the sixteenth century; rich merchants sent their sons to Blundell's School (the old 1604 schoolhouse survives; even in its earliest form, with only two schoolrooms and a dining-hall, it was much larger than Harrow). In 1816, John Heathcoat, driven out of Leicestershire by rioting, opened a factory making lace with his new bobbin machine, and giving Tiverton a new trade which eventually was to replace wool.

Just as at Launceston one rich and worthy citizen decorated his church, so here John Greenaway embellished St. Peter's: and the chapel porch bears the injunction

> *Have grace, ye men, and ever pray*
> *For the soul of John and Joan Greenaway.*

Two bodies, you see, with but a single soul. And their chapel can bear hours of peering: ships sail in stone above the windows, eagles and fish are entangled in the porch; groups of parishioners shelter behind the skirts of saints; wooden cherubs stare solemnly as they support the arms on the door.

As in many Devon towns in the eighteenth century, with so much wood used for building, and so few precautions, there was a considerable fire in Tiverton in 1731, so that the best buildings are almost all of the eighteenth century: several sets of almshouses, for instance.

An exception is the castle, though this is ruined; it was built by Richard de Redvers, and was in the Courtenay family until 1539. Its pink sandstone is anything but 'pretty'—solid and immovable, though a hole was punched in the round tower by a cannon-ball during the Civil War, when Fairfax was attacking. (Later, he used Blundell's as his headquarters.) The sturdy and large gate-house still survives near the ruins of the castle chapel, and near the far from ruined church.

Fire, too, destroyed most of Cullompton, a few miles away, so that only two or three buildings and, providentially, the church, survive. But St. Andrew's is a glory, with an aisle to rival the chapel at Tiverton—unsurprisingly, for it was built by John Lane, a friend and rival of John Greenaway. The Lane aisle has 50 saints to bless its buttresses, and in stone are grotesque animals, monograms, sheepshears, and the astrological glyph for tin. Lane put a memorial inscription rather low along the west wall of the aisle, so that no one should be in any doubt as to who to thank for the gift.

As for the rest of the church, there is a rare clerestory (rare for Devon), and a really lovely panelled wagon roof of 24 bays, carved and coloured; the rood screen is also coloured, though the skulls and bones which originally embellished it are now set apart for separate rumination in the Lane aisle.

Crediton, perhaps the last notable town on the way to Exeter, was the birthplace of arguably the greatest Devonshire man ever born : a large claim, when one remembers the others. But Wynfrith of Crediton, born in about 675 somewhere at the west end of the present town, was indeed remarkable. He was a monk until he was about 40, and always called himself Boniface. He became a teacher, first at Exeter and then at Nursling, near Southampton. There, he compiled the first Latin grammar written in England. In 718 he left England as a missionary to Germany, where he had an enormous effect. He was summoned thrice to Rome by the Pope, who made him a bishop, and later an archbishop.

He was martyred by Freislanders in 754, as he sat quietly reading in his tent while on a missionary journey. Cuthbert of Canterbury shortly afterwards wrote to St. Lull : 'We in England lovingly reckon Boniface among the best and greatest teachers of the faith,' and his surviving letters reveal him indeed as a great and good and lovable saint. He is much better remembered in Germany than in England—even at Crediton—and his tomb at Fulda is still a place of pilgrimage.

Crediton was altogether a religious centre. It had a Saxon Cathedral, and nine Saxon Bishops, before the Vikings drove the see to safer Exeter; and its present church of the Holy Cross, is on Norman foundations: a powerfully dignified building. As for the town itself, it suffered from recurring fires in 1743, 1766, 1769 and 1772; unsurprisingly a lot of the ancient town has vanished, and a few nice old shop-fronts and one or two eighteenth-century and nineteenth-century houses in the typical rich red local brick are all that make it in any way remarkable.

On the road from Crediton to Exeter one passes through Newton St. Cyres, a neat little place with white-walled thatched cottages obviously carefully planned (perhaps by the Lord of the Manor in the eighteenth century, Prof. Pevsner suggests). Above them is the church, unusually and uniquely (in England) dedicated to St. Cyricus and St. Julitta. Cyricus was the three-year-old son of Julitta, who was condemned as a Christian by Diocletian at Tarsus. When the Governor, Alexander, tried to comfort the boy as his mother was removed to execution, young Cyricus kicked out at him and scratched his face, whereupon Alexander threw him down the steps of the tribune, killing him. Julitta, it is recorded, was delighted at her son's martyrdom, and went off contentedly to torture and death.

As with the church at Merton, it is a memorial that attracts most passers-by to this church (though they might spare a glance at the roof of the porch, carved with angels and gargoyle heads, and a family of sow and four piglets). The memorial is to the Northcote family, John Northcote (who died in 1632) presiding in high top-boots and with sword and baton, a skull at his feet. On plaques are the heads of his two wives, and below him his son and daughter-in-law, with their six children, the two youngest in cradles.

Mr. Northcote's two wives have their own inscriptions. Under the first:

> *My fruite was small*
> *One sonne was all*
> *That not at all.*

177

Under the second:

> *My Jacob had by mee*
> *As many sonnes as hee*
> *Daughters twice three.*

Near this monument is another, in miniature, to Sherland Shore, a 17-year-old youth, sitting for ever at his table, cheek leant on his hand, his elbow on a skull, and his violin and mandolins thrown on to the floor, silent at the last.

And now to Exeter: surely the most interesting of all the cities of the West Country beyond Bristol and Bath—the *Isca Dumnoniorum* of the Romans, where the ancient tribal overlords of the Dumnonii reigned after the Romans had gone, leaving their forum and baths to fall and crumble; but leaving also the basic town plan which can still be faintly discerned—for the two roads which cross near the Cathedral (High Street and North Street giving way to Fore Street and South Street) are without doubt Roman in origin (High Street being at the tail end of the Icknield Way).

But there is practically nothing to see, now, of Roman Exeter: a few Hellenistic coins have turned up from time to time; a tessellated Roman pavement was found some years ago, and another during the heavy German bombing of 1942, during which six of the town's churches were destroyed, the cathedral damaged, and thousands of houses demolished. The acres of medieval Exeter which vanished for ever during May of 1942 cleared ground on which were later found traces of the earliest houses in the city, built in the first century after Christ (but what a huge price to pay for minor archaeological discovery!).

The Dumnonii held Exeter as the provincial capital it has always remained, until the appearance of the Saxons; but the next two notable dates in the city's history came with the establishment there of the Bishop's see (removed from Crediton), and the Norman invasion. The first thing the Normans did was, as usual, to build a castle: Rougemont, on the highest point of a red rock above the Exe. Very little of it is left now, apart from the Athelstan Tower and the Norman Gate Tower (which is very comprehensively restored). Exeter's other Norman gateways have vanished completely, though the walls which joined them are visible here and there, many stretches having come to light only after the bombers had cleared away the buildings which had surrounded or covered them.

The most notable medieval building, almost miraculously preserved, is the oldest guildhall in England (its list of mayors is longer than that of London), standing in the High Street, and familiar to everyone who has ever glanced at a book of photographs of old English buildings. It is not, of course, as old as its name: there was a guildhall here in 1160. That original building was rebuilt in 1330, and it would be very odd if its walls at least did not survive within the case of the present guildhall. Mainly, however, the hall is of about 1460, and its arch-braced timber roof is certainly fifteenth century, with the brackets supporting it carved with the arms of Warwick the Kingmaker.

In the 1590s, the portico at the front was added, with the rooms above it supported on pillars of granite; the powerful wooden door and much of the interior panelling is also Elizabethan, and the city arms were carved as a present to the city from the Queen in the year of the Armada.

Here, then, with the Cathedral, were the twin pivots of Exeter life for over 700 years; when Leofric removed his see to Exeter in 1050, the little Benedictine Saxon church became his cathedral, and Edward the Confessor with his Queen travelled west to the installation. After the battle of Hastings, Exeter remained unoccupied by the Normans for two years, with the mother of the dead King Harold living there, a recluse. But then Baldwin de Brionis built Rougemont, and by 1120 Exeter was securely the chief town of the whole West of England.

William Warelwast, a nephew of King William, had become Bishop in 1107, and had started a new cathedral, which remained for a hundred years before a number of bishops turned their hand to it and constructed the mainly Gothic building which is the present cathedral. By this time the nobility and gentry of Devon had their town houses in Exeter; and the town had become important enough to be the sometimes unwelcome focus of political attention. The Bishops began to meddle in politics; some were murdered, others banished. Kings came to visit, and sometimes for particular reasons; during the Wars of the Roses, Warwick took refuge there before flying to France as his cause collapsed. In 1483, Richard III came, and Shakespeare recorded the traditional scene in which he took the name of its castle as an omen:

> *When last I was at Exeter,*
> *The mayor in courtesy showed me the castle,*
> *And call'd it Rouge-mont: at which name I started,*
> *Because a bard of Ireland told me once*
> *I should not live long after I saw Richmond.*

By this time, Exeter's wool trade was fully established; in 1490 the Guild of Weavers, Fullers and Shearmen was established; the town, still small, was becoming increasingly important as a trading centre. But still, incurably fascinated by politics, it was from time to time a centre of disturbance. Perkin Warbeck, marching east to Taunton, forced the North Gate, but was driven off before reaching striking distance of the castle. The King came down a few months later to thank the defenders. A few years later again Catherine of Aragon stayed for a night at the Deanery—her first night in England on her way to a brief marriage with Prince Arthur, and a subsequently more turbulent marriage with his brother.

Probably the most dejecting and violent of all the political and religious rows in which Exeter played a part was the prayer-book rioting of 1549. The rising against the new prayer-book which started at Sampford Courtenay was quelled largely by the efforts of those friends of the King's who had received rich gifts of church property, a little earlier; and there was never any doubt on whose side Exeter was. It held out unflinchingly against attack, despite a complete blockage and consequent shortage of food; only the conscience of one of the rebel leaders, Robert Welsh, the Vicar of St. Thomas, Exeter, prevented the city being fired by red-hot shot.

But Mr. Welsh's intervention did him little good: the King's men inevitably arrived in force to drive the rebels back to Sampford Courtenay, and to defeat them there in battle. Dressed in his Mass vestments, Mr. Welsh was hanged from the tower of his own church.

After the middle of the sixteenth century, life at Exeter became a little less exciting. The Exeter canal, the first in England, was built, and trade increased proportionately; Waldron, Blundell, and the other great wool traders brought vast sums of money to the city, as well as to Tiverton and the neighbouring clothing towns. And Exeter gave a few great men to Elizabethan England—Sir Thomas Bodley, for instance, the eventual founder of the Bodleian at Oxford (whose brother Lawrence, a Canon of Exeter, 'borrowed' many of the cathedral library's books for his brother's foundation), and perhaps most notably Richard Hilliard, the heavenly painter of miniatures, and engraver of the Great Seal of England, of whom John Donne wrote, famously,

> *a hand, or eye*
> *By Hilliard drawn, is worth an history*
> *By a worse painter made....*

In the Civil War, the clothiers were naturally sympathetic to Parliament; Exeter declared for that cause, but surrendered to Prince Maurice within a year, and Queen Henrietta Maria came to the city, and stayed at Bedford House, where Princess Henrietta was born.

Later, Exeter was the first city to be captured by William of Orange after his Brixham landing; and if the citizens were a little cold towards him, being Jacobite almost to a man, they warmed to him later when it became clear that his policy was to encourage cloth trading with the Netherlands. So the last arrival of an invading king passed off, in the end, ceremonially; and ever since, Exeter has been relatively quiet—or was so until its involvement in the 1939-45 war, which brought it the greatest tragedy and the most complete devastation of any of its warring activities.

Although the Guildhall must be one of the best-known buildings in the West Country, it is to the cathedral close and Exeter Cathedral itself that one automatically makes one's way if one has an hour to spend in the city. The roads around the close, within the ancient precincts, are now carparks, and traffic wardens more common than priests, but the whole place still has an atmosphere strong enough to combat the noise and fumes of reversing char-à-bancs, and the twin Norman towers seem unshakable.

If one walks up the nave and around the choir to the Lady Chapel, within William Warelwast's Norman walls, one stands in the oldest part of the cathedral—or above it, for below the Lady Chapel there remains some of the original foundations of the early Saxon church. Bishop Bronescombe, by the time he died in 1280, had begun work on the Lady Chapel, with St. Mary's and St. Gabriel's Chapels on either side of it, and on the choir aisles with St. Andrew's and St. James' Chapels. Then came the outer walls of the present cathedral, and the presbytery, embracing the old Norman apse. By 1304, the presbytery was finished, and work began on the rebuilding of the Norman choir, with its furnishings—including the seats with their misericords, the oldest in England.

Building virtually ended with the death of Bishop Grandisson in 1369, so that the whole of the massive and beautiful building was erected within a century; like Salisbury, it has a unity and consistency of style which gives it an artistic uniqueness among English cathedrals—for Salisbury had been completed in half-a-century, by 1270; Exeter was begun five years later, and was completed within 90 years. A comparison will result in the visitor deciding his preference temperamentally; both are among the finest achievements of English ecclesiastical architecture—Salisbury more austere, Exeter more elaborate.

The west front of the cathedral is not perhaps as impressive as it might be: it lies in a dip which seems, perhaps because of the angle at which the cathedral stands within its close, deeper than it actually is; and while this sets off the whole mass of the building well, it does mean that the west front does not *tower*, and that one seems, even when standing below it, to be seeing it in some strange way from above. But at least one feels closer to Peter, the patron saint, commanding legions of angels and apostles in stone—and prophets and kings, soldiers and priests, with Edward the Confessor, Athelstan, William the Conqueror and King Alfred among them, all with the elongated bodies of the fourteenth century, like the slim lines of Cranach Adams and Eves.

In the thickness of the west wall, as one goes in through the central porch, is the tiny funeral chapel of the great builder, Bishop Grandisson himself—originally a part of the Norman cathedral, maybe, and known then as the Chapel of Radegunde. Preparing it to receive his bones (which are no longer there) the Bishop must have felt he would be standing guard over the entrance to his grand new building.

22 *St Bartholomew's, Lostwithiel: Fourteenth-century font*

23 *Ottery St Mary: boss in Bishop Grandisson's Church*

24 *East Budleigh Church: Sixteenth-century bench-ends*

25 *St Saviour's, Dartmouth: Fourteenth-century south door*

The atmosphere of the cathedral, despite its size, is rather close and almost intimate; the columns, like the ribbed trunks of great oaks, perhaps contribute to this feeling—certainly it is not claustrophobic, but less remote and cold than many cathedrals. The comparison with a wood, easy and hackneyed enough, is one which is nevertheless very striking, and the way in which the columns spread into the very fine vaulting underlines it.

Like some tree-house, high on the north side of the nave, is the musicians' gallery built in the middle of the fourteenth century, its balcony carved with the musicians of the period, playing cymbals, tambourines, bagpipes, trumpets. It has been painted in its true colours, and looks much as it must have appeared when the local minstrels accompanied the hymns.

The choir screen, with the organ perched on top of it, leads into the choir, with its remarkable early misericords. Almost every one of the 51 is amusing and charming: a king sits patiently in boiling water, waiting for salvation; a crocodile cheerfully masticates a man's leg; a man (surely not Lohengrin?) rides in a boat towed by a swan; a knight attacks a leopard; and there is the Exeter Elephant, correct in every detail, except that he happens to have hooves.

The Bishop's Throne is perhaps the finest in England of its period (c. 1314), made by Thomas of Winchester for Bishop Stapledon for £300, and worth every pound. Thomas, who came to Exeter in 1313, sent out to Chudleigh for the wood, and paid £6 12s. 8½d. for it; it lay seasoning for four years, and then Robert de Galmeton, an apprentice of Thomas, was set to work on it, receiving £4 for his labour (with a bonus of 30s. for painting).

The throne rises above the Bishop's chair (with room for chairs for his chaplains at his side), to complex pinnacles over a crowd of wondering animals' heads—monkeys, dogs, pigs, oxen and sheep.

The choir and all its glories narrowly missed destruction in 1942, when a high explosive bomb fell directly on to the cathedral (the only English cathedral to receive a direct hit). It demolished the Treasury above St. James' Chapel, just south of the choir, and destroyed also three bays of the south choir aisle vault. It has all been wonderfully replaced and Herbert Read, a remarkable craftsman, restored the screen which was blown to pieces; the damage is really no longer noticeable. Fortunately, the medieval glass had all been removed to safety, and consequently survived.

The bosses, or knobs which cover the points of intersection of the ribs of the vaults, are particularly worth noticing at Exeter. In the Lady Chapel, these are carved in strikingly realistic representations of roses, vines, hawthorns and oak; and the bosses of St. Paul's and St. John's chapels are beautiful, too.

The Cathedral has some very beautiful monuments—though before mentioning them I ought to draw attention to the exquisite little Coronation of the Virgin painted by some anonymous artist in a recess in the vestibule of the Lady Chapel, in the late fifteenth century.

In the north chancel aisle is a memorial to Bishop Leofric, dated 1072; but do not be deceived, it was pieced together by a number of ingenious gentlemen in 1568. The earliest monument in the cathedral is in fact that to Bishop Bartholomew Iscanus, who died in 1184. There are other bishops remembered here: Bishop Bronscombe certainly received his due in a splendid black basalt monument. This was not carved until the fifteenth century, and is twinned with that of Bishop Stafford. The latter's monument is the earliest example we have of its kind, and became a model for others of the fifteenth century; in 1442, it was copied by the artists at work on Bronscombe's tomb. So here in effigy the two bishops lie, divided in life by 200 years, but under the same noble and complex canopies, in full ecclesiastical dress, and with infinitely delicate detail in the carving which decorates their clothing and surroundings.

The extent to which craftsmen-artists were able to woo stone into subtle forms is reflected again in the lace cuffs of Lady Doddridge, who, reclining on an elbow, lies by the side of her husband Sir John, a judge whose not uncommon habit of sitting on the bench with his eyes closed earned him the name of The Sleeping Judge. He died in 1623. Not far away lies Bishop Stapledon, killed by a rioting crowd in London, while across the aisle is his brother Sir Richard de Stapledon, dignified and cross-legged, pages at his head and feet, one of them carefully holding his horse. Other knights lie cross-legged too, nearby; so do other priests of the cathedral, two of them (Canon Parkhouse and Precentor Sylke) remembered by mournful cadavers which seem to watch one from beneath their shrouds.

'I am what thou wilt be', says Sylke's inscription; 'and was what thou art.'

These are perhaps the main monuments: a touching one which has a beauty probably outweighing the importance of its subject, is the memorial to Matthew Godwin, who died in 1586, and was the organist of the cathedral. He was 18 when he died, and he kneels in profile with musical instruments around him. Sentimental?—perhaps; but at the same time sympathetic.

On the wall of the north transept stands a 1376 clock; although it was thoroughly restored in 1760 (its original works are nearby), its face dates from a period only half a century after the first machine clock was made, and so it is in part at least one of the oldest time-pieces in Europe. Its old face has two dials, one with the minutes, and one with earth, moon and sun, demonstrating clearly that the sun goes round the earth in 24 hours, and the moon round the earth in 30 days.

Finally, the medieval wall paintings: near the clock, above the Sylke Chapel, is a Flemish painting of the late fifteenth century, showing the Resurrection, the soldiers curious or astonished or asleep, the sexton approaching with a spade and his wife with a lantern. Not perhaps among the most marvellous wall paintings of its period, but curiously moving all the same.

The Palace and Deanery are near the cathedral, to the south-east and south-west. The Palace is partly thirteenth century, partly four-teenth; its thirteenth-century chapel was damaged by bombs, but has been restored; it had been damaged or restored (according to one's taste) 60 odd years earlier, when Bishop Temple fell upon it with his architect, Butterfield, and Victorianised it, with white marble cross, rainbow tiles, and a new screen; not entirely successfully. The Deanery is another matter: built on the site of a nunnery (St. Augustine's), with another fifteenth-century chapel, and in the hall a minstrels' gallery.

Elsewhere in Exeter, the surviving churches are almost all inter-esting for one reason or another: St. David's, for instance, is a late nineteenth-century building, extraordinarily romantic in feeling, like a successful Victorian dream; St. Martin's has fascinating fur-nishings; St. Mary Arches is a good medieval parish church; St. Mary Steps, originally right by the West Gate of the city, still has a little vaulted room attached to it which was part of that gate, and outside on the tower wall three powerful little figures in a niche guard a clock dial with the four seasons on it—made by Matthew the Miller and his Sons in the sixteenth century. (Opposite this church, by the way, is a fourteenth-century half-timbered house considerately moved several hundred yards by the workmen building a nearby by-pass.)

There are very few notable private houses surviving in Exeter, thanks to the bombing; one or two in the High Street and in Fore Street, and Mol's Coffee House in the close. Even Georgian Exeter is scarcely to be seen, apart from some houses in the close. And Bedford Circus, the centre of Georgian Exeter, was completely wrecked by bombing. There is Barnfield Crescent, however, and the Custom House (with its good, comfortable brick frontage); Pennsylvania Crescent and Southernhay.

But like Plymouth, the city's showpieces have all too often vanished: how splendid the Subscription Rooms and the Baths must have been, and the other public buildings of the nineteenth century. Still, the Upper Market has survived, perhaps the city's best public building (apart of course from the Guildhall). Its designer was Charles Fowler, an Exeter man who designed many market buildings throughout England, including Covent Garden, and Hungerford Market (which stood where Charing Cross Station now stands). The Exeter Market has a good pediment with strong fluted columns at each end, and a splendid hall with clerestories and sound granite pillars. Really a very fine building—completely utilitarian, completely economical.

It is worth walking down the hill to the old industrial area of Exeter; though so many changes are at the moment being made, so many buildings razed, the land so much altered, that it is dangerous to suggest any particular view: it may have vanished. But here, after all, the life-blood of the city flowed from the sixteenth century onward, and there are many buildings which should certainly be preserved. The Customs House, for example; and the quay itself, a quiet backwater now, from which no doubt many expeditions set out with engineers seeking to make Exeter a larger and more comprehensive port by widening and deepening the waterways. In 1698 William Bailey of Winchester suggested deepening the existing canal to 14 feet, which would have made it unrivalled in its time. He never lived to see his plan in operation, though a new stretch deepened to ten feet was opened in 1725, with the Lord Chief Justice and the Archbishop of York combining to open and bless it.

Water played its part in the construction of another feature of Exeter which is unique and very well worth attention: the network of underground passages which gave the town its water supply, and which can be visited. While there were always plenty of wells in the city, its main water supply came in from the Longbrook Valley, and was piped from a series of springs—including St. Sidwell's spring. That saint is said to have lived in 740, and the spring in question was certainly in use before the Romans came. The passage which brought the water into Exeter is referred to in a document of 1226, but must have been constructed when the Roman Baths (now beneath the Deanery garden) were in use.

Water from St. Sidwell's spring also no doubt supplied the Saxon monastery which stood where the Bishop's Palace now is; in 1347 a new aqueduct was dug, and lead pipes replaced the old stone channels (which can still be seen in places). Other sources were tapped, as well, and the passages constructed in the fourteenth century were certainly in use until 1770, and even after the Exeter Corporation took over the water supply in 1877.

Naturally, with Exeter's long history of intervention in politics and war, the passages were not only used for water. They were certainly heavily guarded in time of trouble, and a few tunnels exist which were unconnected with the water supplies: in 1136, for instance, King Stephen when besieging Baldwin in the castle ordered engineers 'to explore the entrails of the earth' with a view to under-cutting the castle wall.

Visitors can explore some lengths of the passage-ways, and are taken into a large chamber near the foundations of the East Gate, where lead pipe runs still in the old, original stone water-channels; the channels may well be Roman, the pipe may well be of the four-teenth century. Above one's head are manhole covers, and at one point very near the Gate, steps lead down from a now blocked entrance, presumably so that tired travellers could draw water before entering the gate—or perhaps if they arrived late at night after the gate had been closed.

But as far as that larger water-way, the river, was concerned, artificial workings were not much needed, for the river broadens dramatically not far below Exeter, though there was a time when it was dammed at Topsham by the Courtenay family, in order to prevent ships sailing straight past their port and up to the city. That was in 1282, and Topsham had certainly been a busy port for many years before that—since Roman times, if not earlier, for the Romans established a port there to serve Exeter, and drove one of their splendid roads straight as a die to the centre of *Isca Dumnoniorum*, to the Forum. Exeter buses still chunter along where the chariots raced.

The single street connected to the waterfront by alleys running off it, must have been deadly quiet after the Romans left; but sprung into life again in Saxon times, when the village was owned by the monastery of St. Mary and St. Peter. At the Conquest the village became like so much else, the property of the crown, and was shuttled from noble to noble for hundreds of years.

The damming of the Exe succeeded well, as a commercial gambit; though Exeter tried to sue Topsham, merchants were forced to land there, and it was not until the city built its first canal in 1564 that it regained some trade. Even then, the canal's limitations meant that Topsham continued prosperous, and Dutch merchants settled there at the Restoration and built splendid houses for themselves. It is a lovely little town to stroll in, with its churchyard looking over the river from a diminutive cliff, where George Gissing used to sit and 'watch the evening tide come up the broad estuary'. That sad, delightful book, *The Private Papers of Henry Ryecroft*, is set in the countryside around Exeter.

Inside the church at Topsham is an interesting font on which some Norman hacked out a wolf or an eccentric, unhappy dog, with a penchant for fruit (if indeed that is an apple it has in its mouth).

At Clyst St. Mary, not far away, Walter Raleigh, the father of the great adventurer, was walking one Sunday in 1549, when he saw an old lady on her way to church with her rosary. Impatiently (impertinently, one might even suggest) he told her to throw away that tawdry rubbish; the new prayer-book had just come into use, and superstitions such as the counting of beads should be put aside.

The old woman spread the story, and soon a mob set after Raleigh and, as a contemporary account puts it, 'were in such a choler, and so fell in rages with him, that if he had not shifted himself into the chapel' (at Clyst) 'and had been rescued by certain mariners of Exmouth which came with him, he had been in great danger of his life, and like to have been murdered'. Rebels from Clyst joined the others at Sampford Courtenay. Clyst suffered accordingly: many villagers were murdered by the soldiers brought in under Lord Russell to quell the rebellion; Sir William Winslade, who took their part, was hanged in a lane near Winslade House, his home.

Woodbury, the village which lies to the east of Topsham and a little closer to the sea, seems to have taken its name from a nearby Iron Age fort, with great ramparts and a ditch to make it secure, and on a hill looking down over the estuary of the Exe. It has been rather badly damaged by the centuries and by man, but is still impressive; and from the village below it villagers watched soldiers march up to occupy the fort as recently as the end of the eighteenth century, prepared to defend the area against Napoleonic invasion.

Woodbury village itself probably dates from the seventh century, and must have been a pleasant place in its heyday. But man soon put a stop to that, in the person of the Rev. J. Loveland Fulford, a Victorian vicar with a penchant for restoration, who fell upon his little church like a man possessed, knocking holes in the medieval screen so as to present a better view of himself to his congregation, painting over the original colours, and putting in glass more awful than words can adequately convey. Not far away, a little earlier, a local baronet had knocked down the handsome old gatehouse to Nutwell Court, and cut through the roof of its chapel to add a plaster ceiling. All in all, its inhabitants have not done well by the parish.

In the church lies a local dignitary, Sir Henry Pollexfen, endearingly described as 'honest, learned but perplexed'—a judge who prosecuted Monmouth's followers in the west with vigour, and defended the Seven Bishops at their trial.

Nicholas Stone, the most famous inhabitant of Woodbury, was buried in St. Martin-in-the-Fields in Trafalgar Square. The son of a quarryman, he went to London as apprentice to a mason, and became a famous sculptor—after studying under a distinguished master in Amsterdam, and marrying his daughter. At 28, he returned to London and was employed by Inigo Jones on the Banqueting House in

Whitehall, York House Watergate, and the portico of old St. Paul's. He worked in Oxford, too, and became in turn master mason to Charles I and II. Many of his monuments remain, among them the wonderfully restrained one to the Countess of Buckingham in Westminster Abbey. But the most famous of all is that to John Donne, which survived the great fire, and stands still in St. Paul's—an unforgettably impressive carving of the old poet standing patiently, resignedly, in his winding-sheet (in which he had posed to Mr. Stone).

The Borders of the West Country

Until the Napoleonic Wars, Exmouth—at the mouth of the estuary —was simply, like Brighton before the Prince Regent, a negligible collection of fishermen's huts. But then the Continent was closed to the English nobility and gentry, and Exmouth became one of those seaside places to which they travelled instead. Various prominent people became associated with the town; Lady Nelson (poor, sad lady) lived at 6, The Beacon, and Lady Byron at number 19; and other new houses, more or less grandiose, were built at that period— including the self-consciously elegant Grecian bungalow with a Doric front and six free-standing columns. Apart from the good beach, the visitor might stroll out to the east of Foxhole Hill to see The Barn. which if one likes *art nouveau* is a lovely example of it (by E. S. Prior, a pupil of the great Norman Shaw), with shapeless columns and chimneys and big natural rounded pebbles incorporated into the stonework.

In the church at Littleham, a mile or so outside Exmouth, is a carving by Turnerelli showing a woman mourning at an urn; it is in memory of Lady Nelson—a memorial to that disastrous marriage which brought unhappiness both to Nelson and his wife. Well, at least Nelson had Lady Hamilton to console him; the pretty young widow he brought home as a bride from the West Indies, and deserted for the more extrovert, more masculine, certainly more experienced Lady Hamilton, had nobody but a son by her first marriage. They lie near each other in the Littleham churchyard, to· gether with her four grandsons, all of whom died young.

Lady Nelson never entirely tore herself away from her affection for her husband: on their tenth wedding anniversary she was still writing to him as 'dear husband' and 'best of fathers' to her son.

But there were violent arguments; Nelson, sleepless, walked the streets of London, and finally went to live with the Hamiltons, leaving his wife with £1,000 a year. After his death, the Government granted her £2,000 a year, and she settled at Exmouth, paying affectionate visits to her husband's family. Now, it was Lady Hamilton who deserved pity.

Anyone driving along the B3178 from Exmouth to Budleigh Salterton will have a moment of *déjà vu* as he reaches the sea-front of that unpretentious little town. Where has one seen it before? Why, in one of the most famous paintings of its time, Millais' painting of Raleigh as a boy, with his friend Humphrey Gilbert, listening to the stories of an old fisherman. Nothing very much has changed at Budleigh since then; and there is nothing else to remember about the town—except perhaps to spare a thought for James Lackington, who died here in Waterloo year, and who starting life as an illiterate cobbler, opened a cheap bookshop in London which grew to be the first really large one in the country, so that he was able to spend as much as £12,000 at a single book sale.

It was at East Budleigh, a bare two miles from the town, that Walter Raleigh was born, at Hayes Barton, a Tudor farmhouse open to visitors during the summer. Here is the room he was born in, the stairs down which he bumped as a tottering infant; the room in which he did his lessons as a schoolboy, and in the church not far away, where his father was churchwarden, the pew in which he prayed, the Raleigh arms presiding; and within a few feet, a bench-end with a sturdy ship on a stormy sea, with a sailor in its rigging.

This is the place to think of Raleigh, that greatest of English adventurers; if Coleridge was Devon's literary genius, Raleigh is Devon's most admired son—and, like so many of his contemporaries, a complete man—a man of the arts, of sensibility as well as action: historian, geographer, statesman, courtier. From this remote village, he went to London and became one of the most glittering figures at Elizabeth's court, his sharp beard bristling with pride, a lusty lover whose secret marriage to one of the Queen's maids-of-honour brought him into disfavour and perhaps was the first step in his downfall.

Sent to the Tower of London by King James within a year of Elizabeth's death, he spent his imprisonment writing his *History of the World*; after a brief release and an unsuccessful treasure-hunt against the Spaniards, he went again to the Tower, and was executed, unbelievably, as a traitor. 'Your mourning cannot avail me that I am but dust', wrote Raleigh, the realist, to his wife; and on the night before his execution composed one of the finest, most moving poems of the whole Elizabethan era :

> *Give me my scallop shell of quiet,*
> *My staff of faith to walk upon,*
> *My scrip of joy, immortal diet,*
> *My bottle of salvation:*
> *My gown of glory, hope's true gage,*
> *And thus I'll take my pilgrimage....*

If one had to encapsulate Devon's proudest history and highest achievements in one man, Raleigh would be that man; no greater ever came out of the West Country, and East Budleigh is his.

On from the Budleighs to Sidmouth, where in 1820 the Duke of Kent came to die, and where the infant Queen Victoria accompanied him to Woolbrook Cottage (now an hotel). A few years later, the Esplanade was constructed—and indeed building went on throughout the early years of the nineteenth century, much of it charming; there is perhaps no seaside town in the West of England with a more delightful collection of early nineteenth-century houses. But it would be fanciful to imagine that the place had any effect on the infant princess, carried down to the strand in her father's arms. ('She is to be your Queen,' he firmly told passing villagers.)

Ottery St. Mary, five miles inland from Sidmouth, has an uncommonly large church for a village of under 5,000 inhabitants. Bishop Grandisson of Exeter was responsible for this. The original church was consecrated in 1260, and was fairly ambitious. But in 1337, Grandisson converted it into a collegiate foundation with 40 members, and built on to the church a chancel, nave, aisles and Lady Chapel, making it the most important (with that at Crediton) in the county.

Grandisson's church has, like his cathedral, a clock, made in the fourteenth century, which still ticks stolidly away, timing eternity with deliberation, and, one somehow feels, satisfaction. It watched the men at work on the tomb of Sir Otho de Grandisson, with his strangely modern moustache, and his hand on his sword; and that of his wife Beatrice, two angels at her head, two dogs at her feet. It watched the fixing of the brasses to William Sherman, the Elizabethan merchant, and his father and son; and the stone to Gideon Sherman's wife, who died a week after her wedding, 'slipping from bridal feast to funeral bier'.

Fred Thrupp, a sculptor whose very name seems sadly to disqualify him from greatness, turned out the late Victorian tomb of Jane Baronness Coleridge, and the name is echoed nearby on a tablet to John Coleridge, a former vicar of the parish, who married twice and had 13 children. The thirteenth was Samuel Taylor Coleridge.

Coleridge was the one undoubted literary genius Devon has produced. 'The most wonderful man I have ever known,' said Wordsworth; 'the largest and most spacious intellect in my judgement that ever yet existed among men,' said Thomas de Quincey. He spent even his childhood deep among books ('I have read everything,' he wrote to a friend). Opium and a sad marriage marred his happiness—yet what wonderful poems and what wonderful prose he poured forth; and while he very rarely referred to his childhood in Devon, at least once—while at Cambridge—he thought back to his boyish days and remembered the River Otter, on whose surface he skimmed stones: 'Ah! that once more I were a careless Child!'

Thackeray used to spend his holidays from Charterhouse at Ottery, which became the Clavering St. Mary of his fine novel *Pendennis*. And in the church lies the body of William Browne, the author of the long narrative poem *Britannia's Pastorals*, and *Shepherd's Pipe*, and of the justly famous *Epitaph on the Countess of Pembroke*:

> *Underneath this sable hearse*
> *Lies the subject of all verse,*
> *Sidney's sister, Pembroke's mother;*
> *Death! ere thou hast slain another*
> *Fair, and learn'd, and good as she,*
> *Time shall throw a dart at thee.*

At Chanter's House, the Coleridges' home, General Fairfax received a jewel from Parliament as a reward for his conduct of the

Battle of Naseby; and in the great parlour Cromwell and Fairfax signed the Convention of the West.

Honiton, nearby, has returned now, a little, to its former quiet, for a by-pass takes the London-West Country traffic past the town, and the long straight main street (though still pleasantly busy) is no longer one long queue of cars from May to September. This is very agreeable, for miraculously this street retained its unobtrusive calm impressiveness through all the fuss and bother of 30 or 40 years of misuse. There is nothing splendid in it, in the way of architecture; but absolutely nothing unpleasant either, if one excepts the awful ex-cinema at the bottom of the hill.

The street by its straightness signals 'Roman', and indeed there was a settlement here long before the Conquest. Honiton and lace are synonyms, still; but the town was probably one of the earliest in which serge was made, and from the seventeenth century until the end of the eighteenth wool was its mainstay, although Honiton lace had been famous from Elizabethan times.

In the old parish church of St. Michael, up on the hill away from the town, lies Thomas Marwood, physician to Queen Elizabeth I, who saved the life of the Earl of Essex (it was said), and was given an estate in Devon as a reward. His powers of physic may indeed have been remarkable; he himself lived to be 105. The church was gutted in 1911, and consequently is bare of interest. Of St. Paul's, which stands in the High Street, little need be said; it was built by Charles Fowler in the Norman style in the nineteenth century, with as much competence as lack of brilliance.

Axminster and Colyton, to the east, lead us towards Dorset. St. Andrew's at Colyton is worth a visit for the monuments alone: William Westover kneels at a prayer desk with his wife and daughter; so, nearby, do William Drake, his wife and daughter. A tablet remembers John Wilkins, a Commonwealth Vicar so beloved that his epitaph asks

> *Such pillars layde aside,*
> *How can the church abide?*

Margaret Beaufort, wife of the Earl of Devon, a beautiful young girl (her figure only three feet long in effigy) lies on a canopied tomb with angels at her crowned head. In the chantry chapel of the Pole family, Katherine, daughter of the man who presided at Sir Walter Raleigh's trial, kneels with seven children at her side. Her grandson John, not far away, lies with his back to his wife, while two infants sleep in cradles at their feet.

The Great House, in South Street, was the family house of the Yonge family; the house figures largely in the diary of Walter Yonge, a celebrated seventeenth-century diarist.

On the main road from Colyton to Axminster is Musbury, where the Drake family had its origins—and the substantial Drake memorial is the main reason for stopping here at St. Michael's Church. The memorial was set up in 1611 : three couples kneel behind each other, facing east, little windows conveniently placed between them so that each is able to look towards the altar. John Drake and his wife come first; then Sir Bernard, their son (knighted by Queen Elizabeth for his naval prowess) with his wife. Sir Bernard caught a fever at the trial of some Portuguese prisoners (a fever which also slew the judge, 11 of the jurymen, and two other knights who were present). Sir Bernard made a dash for home, but death overtook him at Crediton before he could reach his wife and family, and he was hastily buried there. His son John and his wife are the last couple in the monument —not at all well-carved, but ingenious and telling in its simple piety.

In the same aisle, not nearly so prominent, is a stone plaque to Sir John Drake, whose daughter married a Sir Winston Churchill. She, Elizabeth, held her family home, Ashe House, against the Royalists until it was burned about her, and she was captured and made to march to Lyme Regis as a prisoner. Lyme was under siege, and Lady Churchill was reduced to knitting socks in order to make a crust. But Parliament, after the war, gave her a pension, and she joined her husband in London in the house of an ejected Royalist, until the coming Restoration drove them home to Devon to live uncomfortably in the ruins of their house (of which nothing can now be seen but the fourteenth-century chapel). They had 11 children, the last of whom was to become the great Duke of Marlborough. Ashe House was rebuilt in the 1670s, and is often pointed out as the Duke's birthplace; but since he was born in 1650, this seems unlikely. The Churchills were probably at Great Trill, not far away, at the time.

In Court House, near Axminster church, Axminster carpets were first made in 1755; and brought the town great fame. A hundred years later the carpet business was removed to Wilton, near Salisbury, and Axminster these days is a very quiet little town in which nothing much seems to happen. The church with its steadfast tower, set in the very centre of the town among beautiful yews, is decent but uninteresting. The stirring times for Axminster were really a couple of hundred years after the Minster's foundation in the eighth century, when Athelstan fought at Brunanburgh, nearby, the battle which defeated piratical raiders and made him (as can be seen on his coins) 'King of All Britain'—the first ruler of the entire country.

If one takes a line from Lyme Regis northward, one cuts a corner off Somerset, whose border slopes north-west to the coastline not far from Lynton. So simply for the sake of tidiness, and not because one can in any way define the exact borders of 'the West Country', I propose to speak a little about that wedge of Somerset which lies west of a line not from Lyme to Glenthorne, but from Lyme to Weston-super-Mare. One ought perhaps to include the whole of Somerset in any book dealing with 'the West Country'; and yet while Bristol undoubtedly has the very strongest West Country connotations, Bath has not, and it is only gradually, it seems to me, as one motors down through Wiltshire and then on into Somerset, that one becomes conscious that one has left England and is coming into the West Country proper.

Lyme Regis is, of course, in Dorset, which marches with Somerset for about ten or 15 miles. It remains a virtually unspoiled, very picturesque little town, full of Georgian houses, polite and restrained, with tall cliffs of limestone and shale over a shingle beach, and with a harbour caught in between a jetty on the east and the Cobb, a big curved wall which forms a pier, to the west. Here in 1685 landed the Duke of Monmouth; and here Jane Austen set the unforgettable if unlikely scene in *Persuasion* in which Louisa Musgrove fell, and so confused the mind of poor Captain Wentworth.

Jane herself had come here in 1804 for a holiday with her parents. She swam incessantly, tiring herself out in the warm sea; she danced at a local Assembly, and visited a Mrs. Armstrong, 'who sat darning a pair of stockings the whole of my visit. But I do not mention this at home, lest a warning should act as an example.' No Jane-lover can visit Lyme without thinking of her; Tennyson refused all refreshment when he arrived, demanding at once 'Now take me to the Cobb and show me the steps from which Louisa Musgrove fell.'

Jane Austen got Lyme about right, in fact, and her description (from *Persuasion*) will serve for today:

'The remarkable situation of the town, the principal street almost hurrying into the water, the walk to the Cobb, skirting round the pleasant little bay, which in the season is animated with bathing machines and company, the Cobb itself, its old wonders and new improvements, with the very beautiful line of cliffs stretching out to the east of the town, are what the stranger's eye will seek; and a very strange stranger it must be, who does not see charms in the immediate environs of Lyme, to make him wish to know it better. The scenes in its neighbourhood, Charmouth, with its high grounds and extensive sweeps of country, and still more its sweet retired bay, backed by dark cliffs, where fragments of low rock among the sands make it the happiest spot for watching the flow of the tide, for sitting in unwearied contemplation; the woody varieties of the cheerful village of Up Lyme, and, above all, Pinny, with its green chasms between romantic rocks, where the scattered forest trees and orchards of luxuriant growth declare that many a generation must have passed away since the first partial falling of the cliff prepared the ground for such a state, where a scene so wonderful and so lovely is exhibited, as may more than equal any of the resembling scenes of the far-famed Isle of Wight: these places must be visited, and visited again; they make the worth of Lyme understood.'

Up on the hills behind Lyme is Lambert's Castle, an iron age fort and a round barrow—worth the climb not so much for the site as for the truly magnificent view, to Dartmoor in the west and Cheshill Bank in the east.

At Winsham, over the hills to the north, there is a splendid pre-Reformation painting of the Crucifixion in the village church—torn from the fifteenth-century screen by the Puritans, but carefully preserved for us by the priest and people. Another relic is the paper in which a sheaf of parish registers is bound, for it is composed of pages torn from an illustrated manuscript of *The Golden Legend*, a medieval book of ecclesiastical lore, and the most popular of Caxton's publications. The pages were probably stolen from Forde Abbey, nearby, where a Cistercian monastery was founded in 1138; it has a wonderful collection of tapestries, and 15 acres of fine gardens.

From Winsham the road runs straight to Chard (Forde Abbey is down a minor road to the south), which has seen as much activity over a couple of thousand years as any Somerset town. Roman soldiers marched here; so did the troops of Charles I; so did the army of Monmouth. Judge Jeffreys hung a dozen men at a gibbet in the main street.

The church is all of a piece: fifteenth century, with a Tudor rose on the font. In a side-chapel are the stone figures of Dr. William Brewer, a Jacobean surgeon, his wife, and 11 children—'all men and women grown, and all comforts to them'. William Hitchcock's memorial informs us that Death is the marketplace of a world full of crooked streets, and that

> *If life were merchandise that men could buy,*
> *The rich would always live, none but the poor would die.*

Here too is buried John Stringfellow, a Chard man who in 1868 took to the Aeronautical Exhibition at the Crystal Palace an air machine whose engine, heated by methylated spirit, actually got it off the ground; it flew for several yards. Unfortunately, the methylated spirit lamp kept going out; Mr. Stringfellow returned to Chard and died—but his models are to be seen at the Science Museum at South Kensington, and he was really a brave if virtually unknown pioneer of flight.

James Gillingham, another Chard man, hearing that a man had had his arm accidentally shot off during the rejoicings over Edward VII's marriage in 1863, made a successful artificial limb for him, and started a family business which became famous during the First World War. Chard tends to regard him as a great pioneer in the world, forgetting that metal artificial limbs were being made in Capua as early as A.D. 300.

The glory of Ilminster, a few miles north on the A358 from Chard (but more importantly, on the A303 main London-Exeter road) is the church tower, inspired in the fifteenth century by the tower at Wells. It surmounts a really very splendid church: at least from the outside. Inside, it has been thoroughly ruined by the nineteenth-century restorers; though there is a tomb or two of some interest—that, for instance, of Sir William Wadham, lying in full armour with a lion guarding his feet. His mother, at his side, in widow's weeds, is guarded by a friendly pet dog, with bells on his collar. Nearby lie Nicholas Wadham and his wife, captions emerging from their mouths like balloons in a modern comic: 'Death unto me is advantage,' he says. 'I will not die', she replies, 'but live, and declare the work of the Lord.' Indeed, he did die; and she lived to complete Wadham College as a Protestant institution with a remakably radical outlook (though she was a Roman Catholic).

Broadway, a little village just west of Ilminster, has nearby Jordans, the home of John Hanning Speke, who found (or thought he found) the true source of the Nile, and died somewhat mysteriously in a shooting accident on the day he was to have addressed the British Association on the subject. He was taken to Dowlish Wake, nearby, for burial in a church inhabited by many of his ancestors (indeed from time to time most of them had altered it).

Travel a little north from Ilminster, on the B3168, and you pass the end of Barrington village, with its National Trust showpiece, Barrington Court, as elegant a piece of Tudor architecture as you will find in Somerset. Henry Daubeney, first Earl of Bridgewater, built the house, which fell into virtual ruin within the last century, but has now been brought under the aegis of the Trust to its present state—filled, it is true, with furniture from elsewhere; but with its own linenfold panelling, minstrels' gallery, carved beams, its lovely little dining-room with a traceried screen and sixteenth-century ceiling, its wonderful seventeenth-century fireplaces; and, in the attics, a long gallery in which it was possible to take gentlemanly exercise when the weather was inclement. Beautiful grounds, too, under the sun or umbrella.

But now we are within reach of Taunton, ten miles or so to the north-west: Taunton, which for 12 centuries has dominated western Somerset, first from the earthwork castle set up by King Ine, the King who succeeded Caedwalla in 688. Ine and his kinsman Nun drove back the Welsh, under Gerent, and also repulsed the attacks of Ceolred King of Mercia and the rebel Cynewulf. His violent and valiant Queen, Aethelburg, led a small army against the settlement at

Taunton, and destroyed another rebel, Eadbriht, who had made it his headquarters. From a stronghold there, the King was able to lay the foundations of a united land south of London—a land Alfred and Athelstan were to consolidate still further.

On Ine's castle by the River Tone very little, naturally, remains; at the centre of the present range of buildings on Castle Green the remains of the later Norman castle stand, once occupied by the Bishops of Winchester. Chaucer's son Thomas was Constable here, and the castle stood stoutly for some time—certainly until after the Civil War, for Robert Blake was able at that time to hold out so determinedly against 10,000 King's men that at the Restoration the town's Charter was taken away. Charles II later returned it.

It was in the castle that Judge Jeffreys held yet another of his Western purges. Taunton had greeted the Duke of Monmouth with great enthusiasm in 1658, hung the castle with flags, and presented the hero with a Bible. Three weeks later, Colonel Kirke sat drinking in the White Hart Inn, 30 prisoners from Sedgemoor hanging within his sight in the market place. Three months later still, Jeffreys arrived, and here and at Winchester, with King James' encouragement and approbation, condemned over 300 men to the gallows, and transported hundreds more to the West Indies. The trials were often a mockery of justice.

With rare enlightenment, Taunton has made the castle its museum, with a library of 26,000 books of local interest, several good pictures, and a large collection of bits and pieces illustrating local history from the Stone Age through Sedgemoor and up to the present day.

So out of the castle and, for some fresh air (for somehow the ghostly presence of Judge Jeffreys lingers) up the tower of St. Mary Magdalene, from which (Macaulay said) one may see 'the most fertile of English valleys'. Both churches, St. Mary's and St. James', are handsome, the latter with a Jacobean pulpit around which flirt and scamper seven mermaids, stranded miles inland. How on earth did they come here?

West of Taunton, towards the border, lies Wellington, its name taken apparently at random by the victor of Waterloo as his title. He seems to have known nothing about the place at the time, and only visited it once, subsequently. However, his choice made the townspeople happy, and they demonstrated their pride by planning a 175-foot column, a village of pensioners' cottages, and a statue of the Duke for the top of his column. Alas, the collection simply fell short, and the column is all that remains.

One more warlike connection: a local factory was celebrated for having collected the largest order ever placed in this country for cloth—in 1915, for a million and a half yards of khaki.

In St. Mary's Church lies Sir John Popham, who wears his red robes and the black cap in which he performed one of the two most notable acts of his life: the sentencing to death of Sir Walter Raleigh. He conducted the trial in a notably unjust manner, and one gathers that his presidency at the trial of Guy Fawkes was not marked by any very special judicial qualities. Twenty-six of his relatives surround him on his tomb, with every mark of respect.

Near Sir John is a little stone figure, a memorial to a priest of the church in the fourteenth century, with one of the earliest church inscriptions to have been written in English: 'Richard Persone de Mere [Parson of St. Mary] of Welintone Liggeth in grave. Jesu Christ Godes Sone grawnte him mercy.'

Norton Fitzwarren, nearer Taunton, has a magnificent screen in the chancel of its fourteenth-century church, in which a dragon slopes after a ploughman and team, one sower already disappearing into his jaws. Nearby, another dragon has his eye on a group of men and dogs, while other villagers hide behind bracken fronds and watch.

The Brendon Hills, in the extreme north-west corner of Somerset, reflect a little the roughness of Exmoor, though there are among them one or two charming villages, whitewalled and gleaming, with quiet country churches, unassuming, but with such pleasures as the epitaph, at Brompton Regis, of a young member of the Dyke family, who died at the age of 19:

> *Reader, it is worth thy pains to know*
> *Who was interred here below.*
> *Here lies good nature, pity, wit,*
> *Though small in volume, yet most fairly writ.*
> *She died young, and so oft-times 'tis seen*
> *The fruit God loves He's pleased to pluck it green.*

Northward, a mile inland from the submarine forest fringing Blue Anchor Bay, is Dunster, an unexpectedly fascinating small town. Here, Dunster Castle keeps still a keen eye on the village cluckeying beneath it, the main street running from the castle entrance to a watchtower at its other end, with very much the feeling of a medieval village about it. The houses have been modernised with uncommon tact (the fifteenth-century priory guest-house, for instance, is now three cottages, but its structure is virtually intact), and the whole village has scarcely one ugly or anachronistic note about it.

The church was shared by the local priory and the villagers, and a fifteenth-century screen (one of the most elaborate in the county, with 14 bays of extremely fine tracery) was thrown up by Flemish artists who performed wonders; the fan-vaulting alone is almost uniquely impressive in the West. The church has a fine old solid wagon-roof, with 50 splendid bosses, and in the chantry of St. Lawrence is the monks' old stone altar, with beside it a fourteenth-century processional cross engraved with a portrait of Christ, and with the emblems of the passion, angels, and a pelican.

Dunster Castle was built, as ever, by the Normans (how embattled the countryside must have looked, quite suddenly, in the century after Hastings; previous castles and military encampments were so much more a natural part of the landscape. The Norman castles must have been to the countrymen of England very much what the giant office blocks are to us.) William de Mohun, that great favourite of William, built it soundly, and it stood up to a terrible battering during the dispute between King Stephen and Queen Mathilda, during the latter's supremacy in the West Country. Then, after 400 years of relative peace, it became one of the key points of resistance to Commonwealth forces during the Civil Wars: indeed during the last year of the wars it became the only place in Somerset to fly the Royal Standard. There was a siege lasting for 160 days; but eventually the castle fell.

Three or four miles west of Dunster is Minehead, with Perriton Hill behind it to protect it from the winds sweeping down off Exmoor, and North Hill to keep off the worst Atlantic gales. The old town is charming, with thatched cottages below St. Michael's Church, with its rood loft window from which a lantern guided mariners into harbour, while villagers shared the sentiments carved on the church wall:

> *We pray to Jesus and Mary*
> *Send our neighbours safety.*

Along the coast even farther west is Porlock, with its prestigious, vertiginous hill (drivers from this part of the world laugh hysterically when seeing road-signs promising Steep Hill in the midlands; they really know the meaning of the words). It is a friendly, welcoming little town, and it is perhaps unfair that it is remembered mainly because of the importunate Person who, one day in 1797, walked over to a farmhouse at Culbone, a couple of miles along the coast, to call on a certain Mr. Coleridge. Coleridge had been suffering from an attack of dysentery, and had taken opium for it—which had sent him into a sleep during which, he alleged, he composed the whole of a long poem. Awakened by the visitor, he was kept talking business until most of the poem had vanished, and only the lines which we know as *Kubla Khan* remained in mind. (My own theory is that the poem is as complete as it would ever have been, Person from Porlock or no.)

Apart from the association, Culbone makes a pleasant walk, along a cliff path from Porlock; 400 feet above the growling sea is one of the smallest churches in the West, 36 feet long and 12 feet wide, walls two feet thick, and a window cut from a solid block of stone.

Coleridge loved this north coast, and walked it in the 1790s with Wordsworth and his sister Dorothy; in fact the party walked all the way from Nether Stowey to Lynton, a very considerable distance. They struck towards the sea as soon as possible, and Coleridge, already composing *The Ancient Mariner* in his head, exclaimed as they came to Watchet: 'This is the port from which the Mariner will sail!'—

> *The ship was cheered, the harbour cleared,*
> *Merrily did we drop*
> *Below the kirk, below the hill,*
> *Below the lighthouse top.*

But not only the Ancient Mariner sailed on the waters of Blue Anchor Bay : St. Decuman arrived on a raft from Wales, accompanied by his favourite cow, to be decapitated soon after arrival. Even less welcome visitors were the Danes, many of whom were also decapitated by the Watchetans in a field still called Battle Gore. In the church is a memorial to Hugh Wyndham, a valiant member of a prominent (and pugnacious) local family :

> *He lies beneath this ragged stone*
> *One more his prince's than his own,*
> *Who in his martyred father's wars*
> *Lost fortune, blood, gained naught but tears;*
> *And Earth affording no relief*
> *Has gone to Heaven to ease his grief.*

Nether Stowey, where Coleridge spent perhaps his happiest years, is on the A39 as it runs from Watchet to Bridgewater. Thomas Poole, who became the inspiration for Wordsworth's narrative poem *Michael*, found Coleridge a cottage near the stream running down from Castle Mount, where the Wordsworths spent time with him, and where they all met that dear man Charles Lamb. Poole, a tanner, is buried in the church (surely the setting for the wedding from which the Mariner detained the Guest) under a memorial which confirms Wordsworth's picture of him. It was in this part of the country that the two poets planned *Lyrical Ballads*, one of the few books which have actually and recognisably changed the course of English poetry.

Bridgewater, the major town looking westward to tragic Sedgemoor, is Somerset's chief port, and its presiding genius still, 300 years after his death, is the great admiral Robert Blake, who became famous first as a Parliamentarian General in the early days of the Civil War. His pursuit of Prince Rupert's Fleet and, even more, his defeat of the Spanish Fleet at the Battle of Santa Cruz, marked him for glory : Clarendon said of the last battle, 'all men who knew the place wondered that any sober man, with what courage soever endowed, would ever have undertaken it; and they could hardly persuade themselves to believe what they had done; while the Spaniards comforted themselves with the belief that they were devils and not men who had destroyed them in such a manner'. The Spaniards lost 16 ships and many men; the English one ship, and only 50 men.

Blake died at sea an hour before his victorious fleet entered Plymouth Sound. His body lay in state at Greenwich before a state funeral at Westminster, and it was one of Charles ii's most ungracious (though perhaps understandable) acts to have the body of this hero exhumed and thrown into a pit, after the Restoration. Anyway, he is honoured still at Bridgewater, where his statue presides over the town centre, not far from the house in which he was born (now a museum).

The fifteenth-century screens in the church of St. Mary's are notable; the sixteenth-century one around the civic pew is particularly beautiful, in the same black oak as the magnificent pulpit.

There are some fine houses in the town, too, including one in which Judge Jeffreys stayed during the trials in which he sentenced so many of Monmouth's men to death; and incidentally it was at Bridgewater that Monmouth was crowned by the Mayor, and proclaimed from the castle wall as King. There he stood to look towards Sedgemoor, and from thence he strode off down War Lane to meet his fate.

Only Weston-super-mare and Burnham-on-Sea are notable enough, now, to demand a brief call on our way from the West. Weston was a small collection of fishermen's houses in 1819, when Mrs. Thrale, Johnson's friend, visited it—and could only find two books in the whole place, and those were the Bible and *Paradise Lost*. Now it is a town of 44,000 people, and a vastly popular seaside resort. Burnham is at the other end of the scale: still relatively small, relatively restrained, with staid little hotels and boarding-houses as gentlemanly as you please. There are the two faces of the holiday trade in the West Country: meeting in the middle at the thousands upon thousands of guest houses and bed-and-breakfast houses which can be found in every corner.

But this may yet be the saving of the West Country as a whole: the habit of putting up visitors in private houses rather than (except in the large resorts) large hotels means that the countryside and its ambience can be preserved; or could be if only local authorities would be a little more strict about advertising. Where the West Country has been spoiled, it has been spoiled within the last century, partly by advertising and partly by the network, the cobwebbing, the insane knitting of a tangle of electricity wires, telegraph wires, and television aerials. A very few authorities have kept these under control; but in most places they have been allowed to proliferate, and the result has been that far too much money would be needed, now, to take them down and put them underground, than can possibly be made available.

But this is, really, the one reservation one can make; the spell of the West Country is easy to fall under, almost impossible to shake off. It is a spell as fascinating to millions of people, now, as the spell of the legend of Arthur or of the legend of Lyonesse, that country of milk and honey and untold riches said to lie under the sea somewhere off the West Country coast. In 1780, an old Cornishwoman poured into the sea at Land's End a selection of herbs, and spoke an incantation, in the belief that the land of Lyonesse would rise above the waves at her command. It did not: perhaps because, in a sense, she had it behind her; and one can do far worse than to follow the advice of Hardy:

> *'Tis a May morning,*
> *All-adorning,*
> *No cloud warning*
> *Of rain today.*
> *Where shall I go to,*
> *Go to, go to?—*
> *Can I say No to*
> *Lyonesse-way?*

Index

211

Index

Index

Index